Wine
FOR
DUMMIES®
POCKET EDITION

by Ed McCarthy and
Mary Ewing-Mulligan

WILEY

John Wiley & Sons, Inc.

Wine For Dummies®, Pocket Edition

Published by
John Wiley & Sons, Inc.
111 River St.
Hoboken, NJ 07030-5774
www.wiley.com

Copyright © 2011 by John Wiley & Sons, Inc., Hoboken, NJ

Published simultaneously in Canada

For general information on our other products and services, please contact our Customer Care Department within the U.S. at 877-762-2974, outside the U.S. at 317-572-3993, or fax 317-572-4002.

For technical support, please visit www.wiley.com/techsupport.

Wiley also publishes its books in a variety of electronic formats and by print-on-demand. Some content that appears in standard print versions of this book may not be available in other formats. For more information about Wiley products, visit us at www.wiley.com.

ISBN 978-1-118-13622-5 (pbk); ISBN 978-1-118-13623-2 (ebk); ISBN 978-1-118-13624-9 (ebk); ISBN 978-1-118-13625-6 (ebk)

Manufactured in the United States of America

10 9 8 7 6 5 4 3 2 1

WILEY

Table of Contents

Introduction

• •

*W*e love wine. We love the way it tastes, we love the fascinating variety of wines in the world, and we love the way wine brings people together at the dinner table.

But we're the first to admit that wine people, such as many wine professionals and really serious connoisseurs, don't make it easy for regular people to enjoy wine. You have to know strange names of grape varieties and foreign wine regions. You have to figure out whether to buy a $20 wine or an $8 wine that seem to be pretty much the same thing. You even need a special tool to open the bottle after you get it home!

All this complication surrounding wine will never go away, because wine is a very rich and complex field. But you don't have to let the complication stand in your way. With the right attitude and a little understanding of what wine is, you can begin to buy and enjoy wine. And if, like us, you decide that wine is fascinating, you can find out more and turn it into a wonderful hobby.

Because we hate to think that wine, which has brought so much pleasure into our lives, could be the source of anxiety for anyone, we want to help you feel more comfortable around wine. Some basic knowledge of wine in general — combined with some basic knowledge of the world's most well-known wine regions and the wines they produce — will go a long way toward increasing your comfort level with this amazing beverage.

Ironically, what will *really* make you feel comfortable about wine is accepting the fact that you'll never know it all — and that you have plenty of company.

You see, after you really get a handle on wine, you discover that *no one* knows everything there is to know about wine. There's just too much information, and it's always changing. And when you know that, you can just relax and enjoy the stuff.

About This Book

Wine For Dummies, Pocket Edition, is a wine textbook of sorts, a user's manual, and a reference book, all rolled into one. What does that mean for you? Well, for one thing, it means you don't have to read this book from cover to cover for it to make sense and be useful to you. Simply turn to the chapter or section that interests you and dig in.

Foolish Assumptions

We assume you picked up this book for one of several reasons:

- ✔ You know very little about wine but have a strong desire to find out more.

- ✔ You do know something about wine, more than most people, but you want to understand it better, from the ground up.

- ✔ You're already very knowledgeable about wine in general but realize that you don't know much about the wines of California, France, or Italy.

We also assume that you don't have a lot of ego invested in wine — or maybe you do, and you're buying this book "for your sister-in-law." And we assume that you're someone who doesn't appreciate a lot of mumbo-jumbo and jargonistic language about wine; you're someone who wants straight talk instead.

Icons Used in This Book

Some people are more visual than others. That's why icons are cool. This book uses several icons, and each one has a little tidbit of information associated with it. Here's what each icon means:

Certain details about wine are absolutely worth knowing. If you take nothing else away from this book, we hope you recall the valuable information flagged with this icon.

Advice or information that will make you a wiser wine drinker or buyer is marked by this bull's-eye so you won't miss it.

There's very little you can do in the course of moderate wine consumption that can land you in jail — but you could spoil an expensive bottle and sink into a deep depression over your loss. This symbol warns you about common pitfalls.

Where to Go from Here

Pour yourself a glass and dive into Chapter 1 if you're looking for a crash course in wine basics. For details on wines from some of the world's best-known wine regions — California, France, and Italy — head to Chapter 2, 3, or 4, respectively. If you want to know which wine to pair with tonight's meal, flip to Chapter 5. Or head straight to Chapter 6 for answers to ten of the most common questions we're asked about wine.

For even more advice on wine, from navigating a wine shop to buying and collecting wine, check out *Wine For Dummies,* 4th Edition (John Wiley & Sons, Inc.).

Interested in the full scoop on California, French, or Italian wines? Check out the full-size versions of *California Wine For Dummies, French Wine For Dummies,* or *Italian Wine For Dummies,* all of which were written by us and published by John Wiley & Sons, Inc.

Visit www.dummies.com or head to your local bookstore to pick up a copy of any of the aforementioned informative titles.

Chapter 1

Wine 101

*W*e know plenty of people who enjoy drinking wine but don't know much about it. (Been there, done that ourselves.) Knowing a lot of information about wine isn't a prerequisite to enjoying it. But familiarity with certain aspects of wine — such as the different colors and grape varieties, how to taste and describe wine, the best way to open a bottle, and more — can make choosing wines a lot easier, enhance your enjoyment of wine, and increase your comfort level. You can learn as much or as little as you like about wine. Either way, the journey begins here.

How Wine Happens

Wine is, essentially, nothing but liquid, fermented fruit. The recipe for turning that fruit into wine goes like this:

1. **Pick a large quantity of ripe grapes from grapevines.**

   You could substitute raspberries or any other fruit, but 99.9 percent of all the wine in the world is made from grapes, because they make the best wines.

2. **Put the grapes into a clean container that doesn't leak.**

3. **Crush the grapes somehow to release their juice.**

4. **Wait.**

In its most basic form, winemaking is that simple. After the grapes are crushed, *yeasts* (tiny one-celled organisms that exist naturally in the vineyard and, therefore, on the grapes) come into contact with the sugar in the grapes' juice and gradually convert that sugar into alcohol. Yeasts also produce carbon dioxide, which evaporates into the air.

When the yeasts are done working, your grape juice is wine. The sugar that was in the juice is no longer there — alcohol is present instead. (The riper and sweeter the grapes, the more alcohol the wine will have.) This process is called *fermentation,* and it's a totally natural process that doesn't require man's participation except to put the grapes into a container and release the juice from them.

Now if every winemaker actually made wine in as crude a manner as we just described, we'd be drinking some pretty rough stuff that would hardly inspire us to write a wine book. But today's winemakers have a bag of tricks as big as a sumo wrestler's appetite. That's one reason why no two wines ever taste exactly the same.

The men and women who make wine can control the type of container they use for the fermentation process (stainless steel and oak are the two main materials), as well as the size of the container and the temperature of the juice during fermentation — and every one of these choices can make a big difference in the taste of the wine. After fermentation, they can choose how long to let the wine mature (a stage when the wine sort of gets its act together) and in what kind of container. Fermentation can last three days or three months, and the wine can then mature for a couple of weeks or a couple of years or anything in between.

The main ingredient

Obviously, one of the biggest factors in making one wine different from the next is the nature of the raw material, the grape juice. Besides the fact that riper, sweeter grapes make a more alcoholic wine, different *varieties* of grapes (Chardonnay, Cabernet Sauvignon, or Merlot, for example) make different wines. Grapes are the main ingredient in wine, and everything the winemaker does, he does to the particular grape juice he has.

Local flavor

Grapes, the raw material of wine, don't grow in a void. Where they grow — the soil and climate of each wine region, as well as the traditions and goals of the people who grow the grapes and make the wine — affects the nature of the ripe grapes, as well as the taste of the wine made from those grapes. That's why so much of the information there is to learn about wine revolves around the countries and the regions where wine is made.

What Color Is Your Appetite?

Your inner child will be happy to know that when it
comes to wine, it's okay to like some colors more
than others. You can't get away with saying "I don't
like green food!" much beyond your sixth birthday,
but you can express a general preference for white,
red, or pink wine for all your adult years.

(Not exactly) white wine

Whoever coined the term *white wine* must have been
colorblind. All you have to do is look at it to see that
it's not white, it's yellow. But we've all gotten used to
the expression by now, and so *white wine* it is.

White wine is wine without any red color (or pink
color, which is in the red family). This means that
White Zinfandel, a popular pink wine, isn't white wine.
But yellow wines, golden wines, and wines that are as
pale as water are all white wines.

Wine becomes white wine in one of two ways. First,
white wine can be made from white grapes — which,
by the way, aren't white. (Did you see that one
coming?) *White* grapes are greenish, greenish yellow,
golden yellow, or sometimes even pinkish yellow.
Basically, white grapes include all the grape types
that aren't dark red or dark bluish. If you make a wine
from white grapes, it's a white wine.

The second way a wine can become white is a little
more complicated. The process involves using red
grapes — but only the *juice* of red grapes, not the
grape skins. The juice of most red grapes has no red
pigmentation — only the skins do — so a wine made
with only the juice of red grapes can be a white wine.
In practice, though, very few white wines come from
red grapes.

Is white always right?

You can drink white wine anytime you like — which for most people means as a drink without food or with lighter foods. White wines are often considered *apéritif* wines, meaning wines consumed before dinner, in place of cocktails, or at parties.

A lot of people like to drink white wines when the weather is hot because they're more refreshing than red wines, and they're usually drunk chilled (the wines, not the people).

 We serve white wines cool, but not ice cold. Sometimes restaurants serve white wines too cold, and we actually have to wait a while for the wine to warm up before we drink it. If you like your wine cold, fine; but try drinking your favorite white wine a little less cold sometime. We bet you'll discover it has more flavor that way. (For more on the proper serving temperatures of different wines, see the "Not Too Warm, Not Too Cold" section later in this chapter.)

Red, red wine

In this case, the name is correct. Red wines really are red. They can be purple red, ruby red, or garnet, but they're red.

Red wines are made from grapes that are red or bluish in color. So guess what wine people call these grapes? Black grapes! We suppose that's because black is the opposite of white.

The most obvious difference between red wine and white wine is color. The red color occurs when the colorless juice of red grapes stays in contact with the dark grape skins during fermentation and absorbs

the skins' color. Along with color, the grape skins give
the wine *tannin,* a substance that's an important part
of the way a red wine tastes.

 The presence of tannin in red wines is actually
the most important taste difference between red
wines and white wines.

Red wines vary quite a lot in style. This is partly
because winemakers have so many ways of adjusting
their red-winemaking to achieve the kind of wine they
want. For example, if winemakers leave the juice in
contact with the skins for a long time, the wine
becomes more tannic (firmer in the mouth, like strong
tea; tannic wines can make you pucker). If winemakers
drain the juice off the skins sooner, the wine is softer
and less tannic.

 Red wine tends to be consumed more often as
part of a meal than as a drink on its own.

Thanks to the wide range of red wine styles, you can
find red wines to go with just about every type of food
and every occasion when you want to drink wine
(except the times when you want to drink a wine with
bubbles, because most bubbly wines are white or pink).

 One sure way to spoil the fun in drinking most
red wines is to drink them too cold. Those tannins can taste really bitter when the wine is
cold — just as in a cold glass of very strong tea.
On the other hand, many restaurants serve red
wines too warm. (Where do they store them?
Next to the boiler?) If the bottle feels cool to
your hand, that's a good temperature. For the
full scoop on serving wine at the right temperature, see the later "Not Too Warm, Not Too
Cold" section.

A rose is a rose, but a rosé is "white"

Rosé wines are pink wines. Rosé wines are made from red grapes, but they don't end up red because the grape juice stays in contact with the red skins for a very short time — only a few hours, compared to days or weeks for red wines. Because this *skin contact* (the period when the juice and the skins intermingle) is brief, rosé wines absorb very little tannin from the skins. Therefore, you can chill rosé wines and drink them as you would white wines.

Of course, not all rosé wines are called rosés. (That would be too simple.) Many rosé wines today are called *blush wines* — a term invented by wine marketers to avoid the word rosé because back in the 1980s, pink wines weren't very popular. Lest someone figures out that *blush* is a synonym for *rosé,* the labels call these wines *white.* But even a child can see that White Zinfandel is really pink.

The blush wines that call themselves *white* are fairly sweet. Wines labeled *rosé* can be sweetish, too, but some wonderful rosés from Europe (and a few from America, too) are *dry* (not sweet). Some hard-core wine lovers hardly ever drink rosé wine, but many wine drinkers are discovering what a pleasure a good rosé wine can be, especially in warm weather.

Which type when?

Your choice of a white wine, red wine, or rosé wine will vary with the season, the occasion, and the type of food that you're eating (not to mention your personal taste!). Choosing a color usually is the starting point for selecting a specific wine in a wine shop or in a restaurant. Most stores and most restaurant wine lists arrange wines by color before making other distinctions, such as grape varieties, wine regions, or taste categories.

Although certain foods can straddle the line between white wine and red wine compatibility — grilled salmon, for example, can be delicious with a rich white wine or a fruity red — your preference for red, white, or pink wine will often be your first consideration in pairing wine with food, too.

Pairing food and wine is one of the most fun aspects of wine, because the possible combinations are almost limitless. As you discover in Chapter 5, your personal taste rules!

The Special Technique for Tasting Wine

You drink beverages every day, tasting them as they pass through your mouth. In the case of wine, however, drinking and tasting aren't synonymous. Wine is much more complex than other beverages: There's more going on in a mouthful of wine. For example, most wines have a lot of different (and subtle) flavors, all at the same time, and they give you multiple sensations when they're in your mouth, such as softness and sharpness together.

If you just drink wine, gulping it down the way you do soda, you miss a lot of what you paid for. But if you *taste* wine, you can discover its nuances. In fact, the more slowly and attentively you taste wine, the more interesting it tastes.

 Here are the two fundamental rules of wine tasting: Slow down and pay attention.

The process of tasting a wine — of systematically experiencing all the wine's attributes — has three steps. The first two steps don't actually involve your mouth at all. First you look at the wine; then you smell it.

Savoring wine's good looks

We enjoy looking at the wine in our glass, noticing how brilliant it is and the way it reflects the light, trying to decide precisely which shade of red it is and whether it'll stain the tablecloth permanently if we tilt the glass too far.

To observe a wine's appearance, tilt a half-full glass away from you and look at the color of the wine against a white background, such as the tablecloth or a piece of paper (a colored background distorts the color of the wine). Notice how dark or how pale the wine is, what color it is, and whether the color fades from the center of the wine out toward the edge, where it touches the glass. Also notice whether the wine is cloudy, clear, or brilliant. Eventually, you'll begin to notice patterns, such as deeper color in younger red wines.

The nose knows

Now we get to the really fun part of tasting wine: swirling and sniffing. This is when you can let your imagination run wild, and no one will ever dare to contradict you. If you say that a wine smells like wild strawberries to you, how can anyone prove that it doesn't?

Before you sniff, keep your glass on the table and rotate it three or four times so that the wine swirls around inside the glass and mixes with air. Then quickly bring the glass to your nose. Stick your nose into the airspace of the glass and smell the wine. Free-associate. Is the aroma fruity, woodsy, fresh, cooked, intense, light? Your nose tires quickly, but it recovers quickly, too. Wait just a moment and try again. Listen to your friends' comments and try to find the same things they find in the smell.

The point behind this whole ritual of swirling and sniffing is that what you smell should be pleasurable to you, maybe even fascinating, and that you should have fun in the process.

Hang around wine geeks for a while, and you'll start to hear words like *petrol, manure, sweaty saddle, burnt match,* and *asparagus* used to describe the aromas of some wines. "Yuck!" you say? Of course you do! Fortunately, the wines that exhibit such smells aren't the wines you'll be drinking for the most part — at least not unless you really catch the wine bug. And when you do catch the wine bug, you may discover that those aromas, in the right wine, can really be a kick. Even if you don't come to enjoy those smells (some of us do, honest!), you'll appreciate them as typical characteristics of certain regions or grapes.

Then there are the bad smells that nobody tries to defend. It doesn't happen often, but it does happen, because wine is a natural, agricultural product with a will of its own. Often when a wine is seriously flawed, it shows immediately in the nose of the wine. Wine judges have a term for such wines. They call them DNPIM — Do Not Put In Mouth. Not that you'll get ill, but why subject your taste buds to the same abuse that your nose just took? Sometimes it's a bad cork that's to blame, and sometimes it's some other sort of problem in the winemaking or even the storage of the wine. Just rack it up to experience and open a different bottle.

While you're choosing the next bottle, make up your own acronyms: SOTYWE (Serve Only To Your Worst Enemies), for example, or ETMYG (Enough To Make You Gag), or our favorite, SLADDR (Smells Like A Dirty Dish Rag).

When it comes to smelling wine, many people are concerned that they aren't able to detect as many aromas as they think they should. Smelling wine is really just a matter of practice and attention. If you start to pay more attention to smells in your normal activities, you'll get better at smelling wine.

The mouth action

After you've looked at the wine and smelled it, you're finally allowed to taste it. This is when grown men and women sit around and make strange faces, gurgling the wine and sloshing it around in their mouths with looks of intense concentration in their eyes. You can make an enemy for life if you distract a wine taster just at the moment when he's focusing all his energy on the last few drops of a special wine.

Here's how the procedure goes: Take a medium-size sip of wine. Hold it in your mouth, purse your lips, and draw in some air across your tongue, over the wine. (Be careful not to choke or dribble!) Swish the wine around in your mouth as if you're chewing it and then swallow it. The whole process should take several seconds, depending on how much you're concentrating on the wine.

Taste buds on the tongue can register various sensations, which are known as the basic tastes. These include sweetness, sourness, saltiness, bitterness, and *umami* (a savory characteristic). Of these tastes, sweetness, sourness, and bitterness are those most commonly found in wine. By moving the wine around in your mouth, you give it a chance to hit all your taste buds so that you don't miss anything in the wine (even if sourness and bitterness sound like things you wouldn't mind missing).

As you swish the wine around in your mouth, you're also buying time. Your brain needs a few seconds to figure out what your tongue is tasting and make some sense of it. Any sweetness in the wine registers in your brain first because many of the taste buds on the front of your tongue — where the wine hits first — capture the sensation of sweetness; *acidity* (which, by the way, is what normal people call sourness) and bitterness register subsequently. While your brain is working out the relative impressions of sweetness, acidity, and bitterness, you can be thinking about how the wine feels in your mouth — whether it's heavy, light, smooth, rough, and so on.

After you go through all this rigmarole, it's time to reach a conclusion: Do you like what you tasted? The possible answers are yes, no, an indifferent shrug of the shoulders, or "I'm not sure, let me take another taste," which means you have serious wine-nerd potential.

Parlez-Vous Winespeak?

We have to confess that there's one step between knowing how to taste wine and always drinking wine that you like — and it's a doozy. That step is putting taste into words.

We wouldn't have to bother with this detail if only we could always choose our wines the way customers choose cheese in a gourmet shop. ("Can I try that one? No, I don't like it; let me taste the one next to it. Good. I'll take half a pound.")

"Like/don't like" is a no-brainer after you have the wine in your mouth. But most of the time, you have to buy the stuff without tasting it first. So unless you want to drink the same wine for the rest of your life, you're going to have to decide what it is that you like or don't like in a wine and communicate that to another person who can steer you toward a wine you'll like.

There are two hurdles here: finding the words to describe what you like or don't like and then getting the other person to understand what you mean. Naturally, it helps if we all speak the same language.

The sequential palate

The tastes of a wine reveal themselves sequentially as the tongue detects them and they register in your brain. We recommend that you follow this natural sequence when you try putting words to what you're tasting:

- ✔ **Sweetness:** As soon as you put the wine into your mouth, you can usually notice sweetness or the lack of it. In winespeak, dry is the opposite of sweet. Classify the wine you're tasting as *dry, off-dry* (in other words, somewhat sweet), or *sweet*.

- ✔ **Acidity:** All wine contains acid (mainly tartaric acid, which exists in grapes), but some wines are more acidic than others. Acidity is more of a taste factor in white wines than in reds. For white wines, acidity is the backbone of the wine's taste (it gives the wine firmness in your mouth). White wines with a high amount of acidity feel *crisp,* and those without enough acidity feel *flabby.*

  You can also sense the consequences of acidity (or the lack of it) in the overall style of the wine — whether it's a tart little number or a soft and generous sort, for example. Classify the wine you're tasting as *crisp, soft,* or couch potato.

✔ **Tannin:** Tannin is a substance that exists naturally in the skins, seeds (or pips), and stems of grapes. Because red wines are fermented with their grape skins and pips, and because red grape varieties are generally higher in tannin than white varieties, tannin levels are far higher in red wines than in white wines. Oak barrels can also contribute tannin to wines, both reds and whites. Have you ever taken a sip of a red wine and rapidly experienced a drying-out feeling in your mouth, as if something had blotted-up all your saliva? That's tannin.

To generalize a bit, tannin is to a red wine what acidity is to a white: a backbone. Tannins alone can taste bitter, but some tannins in wine are less bitter than others. Also, other elements of the wine, such as sweetness, can mask the perception of bitterness. You sense tannin — as bitterness, or as firmness or richness of texture — mainly in the rear of your mouth and, if the amount of tannin in a wine is high, on the inside of your cheeks and on your gums. Depending on the amount and nature of its tannin, you can describe a red wine as *astringent, firm,* or *soft.*

✔ **Body:** A wine's body is an impression you get from the whole of the wine — not a basic taste that registers on your tongue. It's the impression of the weight and size of the wine in your mouth, which is usually attributable principally to a wine's alcohol. We say "impression" because, obviously, 1 ounce of any wine will occupy exactly the same space in your mouth and weigh the same as 1 ounce of any other wine. But some wines seem fuller, bigger, or heavier in the mouth than others. Think about the wine's fullness and weight as you taste it. Imagine that your tongue is a tiny scale and judge how much the wine is weighing it down. Classify the wine as *light-bodied, medium-bodied,* or *full-bodied.*

The flavor dimension

Wines have flavors (er, we mean *mouth aromas*), but wines don't come in a specific flavor. Though you may enjoy the suggestion of chocolate in a red wine that you're tasting, you wouldn't want to go to a wine store and ask for a chocolatey wine.

 Instead, you should refer to *families of flavors* in wine. You have your *fruity wines* (the ones that make you think of all sorts of fruit when you smell them or taste them), your *earthy wines* (these make you think of minerals and rocks, walks in the forest, turning the earth in your garden, dry leaves, and so on), your *spicy wines* (cinnamon, cloves, black pepper, or Indian spices, for example), your *herbal wines* (mint, grass, hay, rosemary, and so on). . . . There are so many flavors in wine that we could go on and on, but you get the picture.

If you like a wine and want to try another wine that's similar but different (and it will always be different, we guarantee you), one method is to decide what family of flavors the wine you like belongs to and mention that to the person selling you your next bottle.

Another aspect of flavor that's important to consider is a wine's *flavor intensity* — how much flavor the wine has, regardless of what those flavors are. Some wines are as flavorful as a Big Mac, whereas others have flavors as subtle as fillet of sole. Flavor intensity is a major factor in pairing wine with food; it also helps determine how much you like a wine.

Addressing the Quality Issue

Did you notice, by any chance, that nowhere among the terms we use to describe wines are the words *great, very good,* or *good?* Instead of worrying about crisp wines, earthy wines, and medium-bodied wines, wouldn't it just be easier to walk into a wine shop and say, "Give me a very good wine for dinner tonight"? Isn't *quality* the ultimate issue — or at least, quality within your price range, also known as *value?*

Quality wines come in all colors, degrees of sweetness and dryness, and flavor profiles. Just because a wine is high quality doesn't mean that you'll actually enjoy it, any more than two thumbs up means you'll love a particular movie. Personal taste is simply more relevant than quality in choosing a wine.

Nevertheless, degrees of quality do exist among wines. But a wine's quality is not absolute: How great a wine is or isn't depends on who's doing the judging.

The instruments that measure the quality of a wine are a human being's nose, mouth, and brain, and because we're all different, we all have different opinions on how good a wine is. The combined opinion of a group of trained, experienced palates (also known as *wine experts*) is usually considered a definitive judgment of a wine's quality.

What's a good wine?

A good wine is, above all, a wine that you like enough to drink — because the whole purpose of a wine is to give pleasure to those who drink it. After that, how good a wine is depends on how it measures up to a set of (more or less) agreed-upon standards of performance established by experienced, trained experts. These standards involve the following mysterious concepts, none of which is objectively measurable:

✔ **Balance:** Three words we talk about in the earlier "Parlez-Vous Winespeak?" section — sweetness, acidity, and tannin — represent three of the major *components* (parts) of wine. The fourth is alcohol. Besides being one of the reasons we usually want to drink a glass of wine in the first place, alcohol is an important element of wine quality.

Balance is the relationship of these four components to one another. A wine is balanced when nothing sticks out as you taste it, like harsh tannin or too much sweetness. Most wines are balanced to most people. But if you have any pet peeves about food — if you really hate anything tart, for example, or if you never eat sweets — you may perceive some wines to be unbalanced. If you perceive them to be unbalanced, then they're unbalanced for you. (Professional tasters know their own idiosyncrasies and adjust for them when they judge wine.)

✔ **Length:** When we call wines *long* or *short,* we're not referring to the size of the bottle or how quickly we empty it. *Length* is a word used to describe a wine that gives an impression of going all the way on the palate — you can taste it across the full length of your tongue — instead of stopping short halfway through your tasting of it. Many wines today are very upfront on the palate — they make a big impression as soon as you taste them — but they don't go the distance in your mouth; they're *short.* Generally, high alcohol or excess tannin is to blame. Length is a sure sign of high quality.

✔ **Depth:** This is another subjective, unmeasurable attribute of a high-quality wine. We say a wine has *depth* when it seems to have a dimension of verticality — that is, it doesn't taste flat and one-dimensional in your mouth. A "flat" wine can never be great.

✔ **Complexity:** There's nothing wrong with a simple, straightforward wine, especially if you enjoy it. But a wine that keeps revealing different things about itself, always showing you a new flavor or impression — a wine that has *complexity* — is usually considered better quality. Some experts use the term *complexity* specifically to indicate that a wine has a multiplicity of aromas and flavors; others use it in a more holistic (but less precise) sense, to refer to the total impression a wine gives you.

✔ **Finish:** The impression a wine leaves in the back of your mouth and in your throat after you've swallowed it is its *finish* or *aftertaste*. In a good wine, you can still perceive the wine's flavors — such as fruitiness or spiciness — at that point. Some wines may finish *hot*, because of high alcohol, or *bitter*, because of tannin — both shortcomings. Or a wine may have nothing much at all to say for itself after you swallow.

✔ **Typicity:** In order to judge whether a wine is true to its type, you have to know how that type is supposed to taste. So you have to know the textbook characteristics of wines made from the major grape varieties and wines of the world's classic wine regions. (For example, the Cabernet Sauvignon grape typically has an aroma and flavor of black currants, and the French white wine called Pouilly-Fumé typically has a slight gunflint aroma.)

What's a bad wine?

The fact is there are very few bad wines in the world today compared to even 20 years ago. And many of the wines we could call bad are actually just bad bottles of wine — bottles that were handled badly, so that the good wine inside them got ruined. Here are some characteristics that everyone agrees indicate a bad wine. We hope you never meet one.

- ✔ **Moldy fruit:** Have you ever eaten a raspberry from the bottom of the container that had a dusty, cardboardy taste to it? That same taste of rot can be in a wine if the wine was made from grapes that weren't completely fresh and healthy when they were harvested. Bad wine.

- ✔ **Vinegar:** In the natural evolution of things, wine is just a passing stage between grape juice and vinegar. Most wines today remain forever in the wine stage because of technology or careful winemaking. If you find a wine that has crossed the line toward vinegar, it's bad wine.

- ✔ **Chemical or bacterial smells:** The most common are acetone (nail-polish thinner) and sulfur flaws (rotten eggs, burnt rubber, bad garlic). Bad wines.

- ✔ **Oxidized wine:** This wine smells flat, weak, or maybe cooked, and it tastes the same. It may have been a good wine once, but air — oxygen — got in somehow and killed the wine. Bad bottle.

- ✔ **Cooked aromas and taste:** When a wine has been stored or shipped in heat, it can actually taste cooked or baked as a result. Often there's telltale leakage from the cork, or the cork has pushed up a bit. Bad bottle.

- ✔ **Corky wine:** The most common flaw, *corkiness* comes across as a smell of damp cardboard that gets worse with air, and a diminished flavor intensity. It's caused by a bad cork, and any wine in a bottle that's sealed with a cork is at risk for it. Bad bottle.

A Primer on White Grape Varieties

This section includes descriptions of the most important white *vinifera* varieties today. In describing the grapes, naturally we describe the types of wine that are made from each grape. These wines can be varietal wines, or place-name wines that don't mention the grape variety anywhere on the label (a common practice for European wines). These grapes can also be blending partners for other grapes, in wines made from multiple grape varieties.

Chardonnay

Chardonnay is a regal grape for its role in producing the greatest dry white wines in the world — white Burgundies — and for being one of the main grapes of Champagne. Today it also ends up in a huge amount of everyday wine.

The Chardonnay grape grows in practically every wine-producing country of the world, for two reasons: It's relatively adaptable to a wide range of climates; and the name Chardonnay on a wine label is, these days, a surefire sales tool.

Because the flavors of Chardonnay are very compatible with those of oak — and because white Burgundy (the great prototype) is generally an oaked wine, and because many wine drinkers love the flavor of oak — most Chardonnay wine receives some oak treatment either during or after fermentation. (For the best Chardonnays, oak treatment means expensive barrels of French oak; for lower-priced Chardonnays, it could mean soaking oak chips in the wine or even adding liquid essence of oak.) Except for Northeastern Italy and France's Chablis and Mâconnais districts,

where oak usually isn't used for Chardonnay,
oaky Chardonnay wine is the norm and unoaked
Chardonnay is the exception.

Chardonnay itself has fruity aromas and flavors that
range from apple — in cooler wine regions — to tropi-
cal fruits, especially pineapple, in warmer regions.
Chardonnay also can display subtle earthy aromas,
such as mushroom or minerals. Chardonnay wine has
medium to high acidity and is generally full-bodied.
Classically, Chardonnay wines are dry. But most
inexpensive Chardonnays these days are actually a
bit sweet.

Chardonnay is a grape that can stand on its own in a
wine, and the top Chardonnay-based wines (except
for Champagne and similar bubblies) are 100-percent
Chardonnay. But less-expensive wines that are labeled
Chardonnay — those selling for less than $10 a bottle
in the United States, for example — are likely to have
some other, far less distinguished grape blended in, to
help reduce the cost of making the wine.

Riesling

The great Riesling wines of Germany have put the
Riesling grape on the charts as an undisputedly noble
variety. Riesling shows its real class only in a few
places outside of Germany, however. The Alsace
region of France, Austria, and the Clare Valley region
of Australia are among the few.

Riesling wines are far less popular today than
Chardonnay. Maybe that's because Riesling is the
antithesis of Chardonnay. Whereas Chardonnay is
usually gussied up with oak, Riesling almost never is;
whereas Chardonnay can be full-bodied and rich,
Riesling is more often light-bodied, crisp, and refreshing. Riesling's fresh, vivid personality can make many
Chardonnays taste clumsy in comparison.

The common perception of Riesling wines is that they're sweet, and many of them are — but plenty of them aren't. Alsace Rieslings are normally dry, many German Rieslings are fairly dry, and a few American Rieslings are dry. (Riesling can be vinified either way, according to the style of wine a producer wants to make.) Look for the word *trocken* (meaning dry) on German Riesling labels and the word *dry* on American labels if you prefer the dry style of Riesling.

High acidity, low to medium alcohol levels, and aromas/flavors that range from ebulliently fruity to flowery to minerally are trademarks of Riesling.

 Riesling wines are sometimes labeled as *White Riesling* or *Johannisberg Riesling* — both synonyms for the noble Riesling grape. With wines from Eastern European countries, though, read the fine print: Olazrizling, Laskirizling, and Welschriesling are from another grape altogether.

Sauvignon Blanc

Sauvignon Blanc is a white variety with a very distinctive character. It's high in acidity with pronounced aromas and flavors. Besides herbaceous character (sometimes referred to as *grassy*), Sauvignon Blanc wines display mineral aromas and flavors, vegetal character, or — in certain climates — fruity character, such as ripe melon, figs, or passion fruit. The wines are light- to medium-bodied and usually dry. Most of them are unoaked, but some are oaky.

France has two classic wine regions for the Sauvignon Blanc grape: Bordeaux; and the Loire Valley, where the two best-known Sauvignon wines are called Sancerre or Pouilly-Fumé. In Bordeaux, Sauvignon Blanc is sometimes blended with Sémillon; some of the wines that are blended about 50-50 from the two grapes and fermented in oak are among the great white wines of the world.

Sauvignon Blanc is also important in northeastern Italy, South Africa, and parts of California, where the wines are sometimes labeled as "Fumé Blanc." New Zealand's Sauvignon Blanc wines in particular are renowned for their fresh, flavorful style.

Pinot Gris/Pinot Grigio

Pinot Gris (*gree*) is one of several grape varieties called Pinot: Pinot Blanc (white Pinot), Pinot Noir (black Pinot), Pinot Meunier (we don't know how that one translates), and Pinot Gris (gray Pinot), which is called *Pinot Grigio* in Italian. Pinot Gris is believed to have mutated from the black Pinot Noir grape. Although it's considered a white grape, its skin color is unusually dark for a white variety.

Wines made from Pinot Gris can be deeper in color than most white wines — although most of Italy's Pinot Grigio wines are quite pale. Pinot Gris wines are medium- to full-bodied, usually not oaky, and have rather low acidity and fairly neutral aromas. Sometimes the flavor and aroma can suggest the skins of fruit, such as peach skins or orange rind.

Pinot Gris is an important grape throughout northeastern Italy, and it also grows in Germany, where it's called Ruländer. The only region in France where Pinot Gris is important is in Alsace, where it really struts its stuff. Oregon has had good success with Pinot Gris, and more and more winemakers in California are now taking a shot at it. Because Pinot Grigio is one of the best-selling inexpensive white wines in the United States, countries such as Chile and Australia now grow this grape for mass-market wines, and they often call the wine "Pinot Grigio."

A Primer on Red Grape Varieties

Here are descriptions of important red *vinifera* grape
varieties. You'll encounter these grapes in varietal
wines and also in place-name wines.

Cabernet Sauvignon

Cabernet Sauvignon is a noble grape variety that
grows well in just about any climate that isn't very
cool. It became famous through the age-worthy red
wines of the Médoc district of Bordeaux (which usually also contain Merlot and Cabernet Franc, in vary-
ing proportions). But today California is an equally
important region for Cabernet Sauvignon — not to
mention Washington, southern France, Italy,
Australia, South Africa, Chile, and Argentina.

The Cabernet Sauvignon grape makes wines that are
high in tannin and are medium- to full-bodied. The
textbook descriptor for Cabernet Sauvignon's aroma
and flavor is *black currants* or *cassis;* the grape can
also contribute vegetal tones to a wine when or where
the grapes are less than ideally ripe.

Cabernet Sauvignon wines come in all price
and quality levels. The least-expensive versions
are usually fairly soft and very fruity, with
medium body. The best wines are rich and firm
with great depth and classic Cabernet flavor.
Serious Cabernet Sauvignons can age for
15 years or more.

Because Cabernet Sauvignon is fairly tannic (and
because of the blending precedent in Bordeaux),
winemakers often blend it with other grapes; usually
Merlot — being less tannic — is considered an ideal
partner. Australian winemakers have an unusual practice of blending Cabernet Sauvignon with Syrah.

Merlot

Deep color, full body, high alcohol, and low tannin are the characteristics of wines made from the Merlot grape. The aromas and flavors can be plummy or sometimes chocolatey, or they can suggest tea leaves.

 Some wine drinkers find Merlot easier to like than Cabernet Sauvignon because it's less tannic. (But some winemakers feel that Merlot isn't satisfactory in its own right and, thus, often blend it with Cabernet Sauvignon, Cabernet Franc, or both.) Merlot makes both inexpensive, simple wines and, when grown in the right conditions, very serious wines.

Merlot is actually the most-planted grape variety in Bordeaux, where it excels in the Right Bank districts of Pomerol and St. Emilion. Merlot is also important in Washington, California, the Long Island district of New York, northeastern Italy, and Chile.

Pinot Noir

Pinot Noir is finicky, troublesome, enigmatic, and challenging. But a great Pinot Noir can be one of the greatest wines ever.

The prototype for Pinot Noir wine is red Burgundy, from France, where tiny vineyard plots yield rare treasures of wine made entirely from Pinot Noir. Oregon, California, New Zealand, and parts of Australia and Chile also produce good Pinot Noir. But Pinot Noir's production is rather limited, because this variety is very particular about climate and soil.

Pinot Noir wine is lighter in color than Cabernet or Merlot. It has relatively high alcohol, medium to high acidity, and medium to low tannin (although oak barrels can contribute additional tannin to the wine). Its

flavors and aromas can be very fruity — often like a
mélange of red berries — or earthy and woodsy,
depending on how it's grown and/or vinified. Pinot
Noir is rarely blended with other grapes.

Syrah/Shiraz

The northern part of France's Rhône Valley is the
classic home for great wines from the Syrah grape.
Rhône wines such as Hermitage and Côte-Rôtie are
the inspiration for Syrah's dissemination to Australia,
California, Washington, Italy, and Spain.

Syrah produces deeply colored wines with full body,
firm tannin, and aromas/flavors that can suggest berries, smoked meat, black pepper, tar, or even burnt
rubber (believe it or not). In Australia, Syrah (called
Shiraz) comes in several styles — some of them
charming, medium-bodied, vibrantly fruity wines that
are quite the opposite of the Northern Rhône's powerful Syrahs.

Syrah doesn't require any other grape to complement
its flavors, although in Australia it's often blended
with Cabernet, and in the Southern Rhône it's often
part of a blended wine with Grenache and other
varieties.

Zinfandel

White Zinfandel is such a popular wine — and so much
better known than the red style of Zinfandel — that its
fans might argue that Zinfandel is a white grape. But
it's really red.

Zin — as lovers of red Zinfandel call it — makes rich,
dark wines that are high in alcohol and medium to
high in tannin. They can have a blackberry or raspberry aroma and flavor, a spicy or tarry character,

or even a jammy flavor. Some Zins are lighter than others and meant to be enjoyed young, and some are serious wines with a tannin structure that's built for aging. (You can tell which is which by the price.)

Nebbiolo

Outside of scattered sites in northwestern Italy — mainly the Piedmont region — Nebbiolo just doesn't make remarkable wine. But the extraordinary quality of Barolo and Barbaresco, two Piedmont wines, prove what greatness it can achieve under the right conditions.

The Nebbiolo grape is high in both tannin and acid, which can make a wine tough. Fortunately, it also gives enough alcohol to soften the package. Its color can be deep when the wine is young but can develop orangey tinges within a few years. Its complex aroma is fruity (strawberry, cherry), earthy and woodsy (tar, truffles), herbal (mint, eucalyptus, anise), and floral (roses).

Lighter versions of Nebbiolo are meant to be drunk young — wines labeled Nebbiolo d'Alba, Roero, or Nebbiolo delle Langhe, for example. Barolo and Barbaresco are wines that deserve a *minimum* of eight years of age before drinking.

Sangiovese

This Italian grape has proven itself in the Tuscany region of Italy, especially in the Brunello di Montalcino and Chianti districts. Sangiovese makes wines that are medium to high in acidity and firm in tannin; the wines can be light-bodied to full-bodied, depending on exactly where the grapes grow and how the wine is made. The aromas and flavors of the wines are fruity — especially cherry, often tart cherry — with floral nuances of violets and sometimes a slightly nutty character.

Tempranillo

Tempranillo is Spain's candidate for greatness. It gives wines deep color, low acidity, and only moderate alcohol. Modern renditions of Tempranillo from the Ribera del Duero region and elsewhere in Spain prove what color and fruitiness this grape has. In more traditional wines, such as those of the Rioja region, much of the grape's color and flavor is lost due to long wood aging and to blending with varieties that lack color, such as Grenache.

Getting the Cork Out

Before you can even think about removing the cork from a wine bottle, you need to deal with whatever covers the cork. Most wine bottles have a colorful covering over the top of the bottle that's called a *capsule*. Wineries place capsules on top of corks for two reasons: to keep the corks clean and to create a fetching look for their bottles.

Whether the capsule is plastic, foil, or cellophane, remove the entire capsule so that no wine can possibly come into contact with the covering when you pour. (Use the small knife that's part of most *corkscrews* — the devices that exist solely for opening wine bottles.) When you encounter a plastic plug atop the cork rather than a capsule, just flick it off with the tip of a knife.

After removing the capsule or plug, wipe the top of the bottle clean with a damp cloth. Sometimes the visible end of the cork is dark with mold that developed under the capsule; in that case, wipe all the more diligently. (If you encounter mold atop the cork, don't be concerned. That mold is actually a good sign: It means the wine has been stored in humid conditions.)

The corkscrew not to use

The one corkscrew we absolutely avoid happens to be the most common type of corkscrew around. We don't like it for one very simple reason: It mangles the cork, almost guaranteeing that brown flakes will be floating in your glass of wine.

That corkscrew is the infamous wing-type corkscrew, a bright silver-colored, metal device that looks like a cross between a pair of pliers and a drill; when you insert this corkscrew into a cork, two "wings" open out from the side of the corkscrew. The major shortcoming of this device is its very short worm, or *auger* (the curly prong that bores into the cork), which is too short for many corks and overly aggressive on all of them.

 Invest a few dollars in a decent corkscrew right off the bat. The time and hassle you'll save will be more than worth the investment.

The corkscrew to buy

 The one indispensable corkscrew for every household is the Screwpull. It was invented in the early 1980s by a renowned Houston scientist, Dr. Herbert Allen, who was apparently tired of having a 10-cent piece of cork get the better of him.

The Screwpull is about 6 inches long. It consists of an arched piece of plastic (which looks like a clothespin on steroids) straddling an inordinately long, 5-inch worm that's coated with Teflon (see Figure 1-1).

To use this corkscrew, you simply place the plastic over the bottle top (having already removed the capsule), until a lip on the plastic is resting on the top of the bottle. Insert the worm through the plastic until it touches the cork. Hold on to the plastic firmly while turning the lever atop the worm clockwise. The worm descends into the cork. Then you simply keep turning the lever in the same clockwise direction, and the cork magically emerges from the bottle. To remove the cork from the Screwpull, simply turn the lever counterclockwise while holding on to the cork.

The Screwpull comes in many colors and costs about $20 in wine shops, kitchen stores, and specialty catalogs. It's very simple to use, doesn't require a lot of muscle, and is our corkscrew of choice for most of the corks that we encounter.

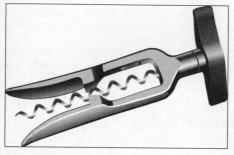

© Akira Chiwaki
Figure 1-1: The Screwpull corkscrew.

The Screwpull has one drawback; because it's made of plastic, it can break. But now a stainless steel version is available, for about $30. This Screwpull should last indefinitely.

A special case: Opening Champagne and sparkling wine

Opening a bottle of sparkling wine is usually an exciting occasion. Who doesn't enjoy the ceremony of a cold glass of bubbly? But you need to use a completely different technique than you'd use to open a regular wine bottle. The cork even looks different. Sparkling wine corks have a mushroom-shape head that protrudes from the bottle and a wire cage that holds the cork in place against the pressure that's trapped inside the bottle.

Never, ever use a corkscrew on a bottle of sparkling wine. The pressure of the trapped carbonation, when suddenly released, can send the cork *and* corkscrew flying right into your eye.

Forget how they do it in locker rooms

If your bottle of bubbly has just traveled, let it rest for a while, preferably a day. Controlling the cork is difficult when the carbonation has been stirred up. (Hey, you wouldn't open a large bottle of soda that's warm and shaken up, either, would you? Sparkling wine has much more carbonated pressure than soda, and it needs more time to settle down.)

If you're in the midst of a sparkling-wine emergency and need to open the bottle anyway, one quick solution is to calm down the carbonation by submerging the bottle in an ice bucket for about 30 minutes. (Fill the bucket with one-half ice cubes and one-half ice-cold water.)

In any case, be careful when you remove the wire cage, and keep one hand on top of the cork as a precaution. (We had a hole in our kitchen ceiling from one adventure with a flying cork.) Be sure to point the bottle away from people and other fragile objects.

A sigh is better than a pop

Removing the cork from sparkling wine with just a gentle sigh rather than a loud pop is fairly easy.

Simply hold the bottle at a 45-degree angle with a towel wrapped around it if it's wet. (Try resting the base of the bottle on your hipbone.) Twist the bottle while holding onto the cork so you can control the cork as it emerges. When you feel the cork starting to come out of the bottle, *push down against the cork* with some pressure, as if you don't want to let it out of the bottle. In this way, the cork will emerge slowly with a hiss or sigh sound rather than a pop.

Every once in a while, you'll come across a really tight sparkling-wine cork that doesn't want to budge. Try either running the top of the bottle under warm water for a few minutes or wrapping a towel around the cork to create friction. Either action will usually make it possible for you to remove the cork.

Not Too Warm, Not Too Cold

Serving wine at the ideal temperature is a vital factor in your enjoyment of wine. Frequently, we've tasted the same wine at different temperatures and have loved the wine on one occasion but disliked it the other!

Just as many red wines are served too warm, most white wines are definitely served too cold, judging by the service that we've received in many restaurants. The higher the quality of a white wine, the less cold it should be, so that you can properly appreciate its flavor.

Here are our recommended serving temperatures for various types of wines:

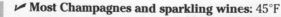 **Most Champagnes and sparkling wines:** 45°F

Older or expensive, complex Champagnes: 52°F–54°F

- ✔ **Inexpensive sweet wines:** 50°F–55°F

- ✔ **Rosés and blush wines:** 50°F–55°F

- ✔ **Simpler, inexpensive, quaffing-type white wines:** 50°F–55°F

- ✔ **Dry Sherry, such as fino or manzanilla:** 55°F–56°F

- ✔ **Fine, dry white wines:** 58°F–62°F

- ✔ **Finer dessert wines, such as a good Sauternes:** 58°F–62°F

- ✔ **Light, fruity red wines:** 58°F–60°F

- ✔ **Most red wines:** 62°F–65°F

- ✔ **Sherry (other than dry fino or manzanilla):** 62°F–65°F

- ✔ **Port:** 62°F–65°F

 Are you wondering how to know when your bottle is the right temperature? Just feel the bottle with your hand and take a guess. Practice makes perfect.

Keeping Leftover Wine

A sparkling-wine stopper, a device that fits over an opened bottle, is really effective in keeping any remaining Champagne or sparkling wine fresh (often for several days) in the refrigerator. But what do you do when you have red or white wine left in the bottle?

You can put the cork back in the bottle if it still fits, and put the bottle into the refrigerator. (Even red wines will stay fresher there; just take the bottle out to warm up about an hour before serving it.) But four other methods are also reliable in keeping your remaining wine from oxidizing; these techniques are all the more effective if you put the bottle in the fridge after using them:

- ✔ If you have about half a bottle of wine left, simply pour the wine into a clean, empty half-sized wine bottle and recork the smaller bottle. We sometimes buy wines in half-bottles, just to make sure we have the empty half-bottles around.

- ✔ Use a handy, inexpensive, miniature pump called a Vac-U-Vin found in most wine stores. This pump removes oxygen from the bottle, and the rubber stoppers that come with it prevent additional oxygen from entering the bottle. It's supposed to keep your wine fresh for up to a week, but it doesn't always work that well, in our experience.

- ✔ Buy small cans of inert gas in some wine stores. Just squirt a few shots of the gas into the bottle through a skinny straw, which comes with the can, and put the cork back in the bottle. The gas displaces the oxygen in the bottle, thus protecting the wine from oxidizing. Simple and effective. Private Preserve is a good brand and highly recommended.

- ✔ A newer device, called WineSavor, is a flexible plastic disk that you roll up and insert down the bottle's neck. Once inside the bottle, the disk opens up and floats on top of the wine, blocking the wine from oxygen.

To avoid all this bother, just drink the wine! Or, if you're not too fussy, just place the leftover wine in the refrigerator and drink it in the next day or two — before it goes into a coma.

Chapter 2

Touring California Wine Country

. . . .

In This Chapter

▶ Identifying which areas produce the best wine

▶ Getting to know California's wine regions

▶ Discovering top producers and their recommended wines

. . . .

*B*efore 1970, only a few dozen operating wineries existed in California; today, the state has well over 800 bonded wineries (about a dozen or so "giants," but mainly small, family-owned operations). California's growth has stimulated interest in wine all across the United States. Today, wineries exist in all 50 states. And California is the largest wine-producing state, by far. This chapter introduces you to California's wine regions and provides you with recommended wines from each one.

California, USA

When most wine drinkers think about American wine, they think of California. That's not surprising — the wines of California make up about 88 percent of U.S. wine production.

Reading an American wine label

The name of the grape a wine is made from has more importance on a U.S. wine label than the name of the region where the wine was produced. Wines labeled with the name of a grape variety in the United States must contain at least 75 percent of that grape variety. Wines with an AVA indication must be made at least 85 percent from grapes from that viticultural area. Wines with vintage years must derive at least 85 percent from the named vintage.

Keep in mind that the words *reserve, special selection, private reserve, barrel select, vintners reserve, classic,* and so on have no legal definition in the United States. Although many premium wineries use these terms to indicate their special or better wines, most of the larger wineries use the same terms on their inexpensive bottlings as marketing tools.

Where California wines grow

In sunny California, there's no lack of warm climate for growing grapes. For fine wine production, the challenge is finding areas that are cool enough, with poor enough soil, so the grapes don't ripen too quickly, too easily, without full flavor development. Nearness to the Pacific Coast and higher altitudes assure cooler climates more so than latitude does. Fine wines, therefore, come from vineyards up and down almost the whole length of the state.

The most important fine wine areas and districts in California are as follows (see Figure 2-1):

✔ **North Coast:**
- Napa Valley
- Sonoma County
- Mendocino and Lake counties

✔ **North-Central Coast:**
- Livermore and Santa Clara valleys (San Francisco Bay Area)
- Santa Cruz Mountains
- Monterey County

✔ **Sierra Foothills**

✔ **South-Central Coast:**
- San Luis Obispo County
- Santa Barbara County

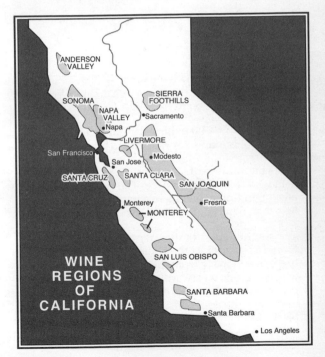

© Akira Chiwaki

Figure 2-1: The wine regions of California.

When the wines are good

Weather variations from year to year are far less dramatic in California than they are in most European wine regions. One major reason is that rain doesn't fall during the growing season in much of California. (Rain at the wrong time is the usual cause of Europe's poorer vintages.) Using irrigation, winemakers, in effect, control the water to the vines. Ironically, one factor that can cause vintage variation in California is lack of water for irrigation due to drought.

Napa Valley: As Tiny As It Is Famous

The part of California Wine Country that's most famous is, without a doubt, the North Coast. When you think of California wine, you likely think of Napa Valley.

Located about a 90-minute drive northeast of San Francisco, Napa Valley is home to many of California's most prestigious wineries — and certainly its most expensive vineyard land. About 240 wineries have managed to find space here. The region's size is actually much tinier than its reputation: Napa produces less than 5 percent of California's wine grapes.

The southern part of the valley, especially the Carneros district, is the coolest area, thanks to ocean breezes and mists from the San Pablo Bay. Carneros — which extends westward into Sonoma County — has become the vineyard area of choice for grape varieties that enjoy the cool climate: Chardonnay, Pinot Noir, Merlot, and grapes for sparkling wines. North toward Calistoga — away from the bay influence — the climate gets quite hot (but always with cool nights).

Wineries and vineyards occupy almost every part of Napa Valley. Many vineyards are on the valley floor, some are in the hills and mountains to the west (the Mayacamas Mountains), and some are in the mountains to the east (especially Howell Mountain). Napa winemakers and grape growers have established 15 *American Viticultural Areas* (AVAs; the names of the regions of production) besides the broad Napa Valley AVA itself and the even broader (six-county) North Coast AVA:

- ✔ Spring Mountain, Diamond Mountain, and Mount Veeder (all in the western mountains)
- ✔ Howell Mountain, Stags Leap District, and Atlas Peak (all hilly or mountainous areas in eastern Napa Valley)
- ✔ Chiles Valley (in the easternmost part of Napa Valley)
- ✔ Oak Knoll District, Yountville, Oakville, Rutherford, and St. Helena (from south to north on the valley floor)
- ✔ Wild Horse Valley (in southeastern Napa Valley)
- ✔ Los Carneros (part in Napa Valley, part in Sonoma)
- ✔ Calistoga (in northwestern Napa Valley)

The grapes of Napa

Almost everyone in Napa who makes table wine makes a Cabernet Sauvignon and a Chardonnay, and many Napa producers now also make Merlot.

The six most important wines in Napa are two whites — Chardonnay and Sauvignon Blanc (often labeled Fumé Blanc) — and four reds — Cabernet Sauvignon, Merlot, Pinot Noir (mainly from cool Carneros), and Zinfandel.

But blended wines have become increasingly important in the last 15 years. If red, these blends are usually made from red Bordeaux varieties (Cabernet Sauvignon, Cabernet Franc, Merlot, and sometimes even Malbec and Petit Verdot). If white, they're usually made from the white Bordeaux grapes (Sauvignon Blanc and Sémillon).

Who's who in Napa (and for what)

If just about every winery in Napa makes a Chardonnay and a Cabernet Sauvignon, how can you distinguish the wineries from one another? Good question — with no easy answer. The following alphabetical list indicates some of the better wine producers in Napa Valley, as well as their best wines, and can help steer you in the right direction. We know the list looks overwhelming, but . . . that's Napa! (**Note:** Our list includes Napa classics as well as some personal favorites.)

Although all the wineries in the following list are situated in Napa Valley, their wines aren't necessarily always made with Napa-grown grapes; the geographic name on the label tells you where the grapes came from.

✔ **Acacia Winery:** Pinot Noir, Chardonnay

✔ **Anderson's Conn Valley:** Cabernet Sauvignon, Chardonnay

✔ **Araujo Estate:** Cabernet Sauvignon (Eisele Vineyard), Syrah

✔ **Beaulieu Vineyard:** Cabernet Sauvignon Private Reserve (Georges de Latour), Cabernet Sauvignon (Rutherford)

✔ **Beringer Vineyards:** Cabernet Sauvignon (single-vineyard wines), Chardonnay Private Reserve, Merlot (Bancroft Ranch)

✔ **Bryant Family Vineyard:** Cabernet Sauvignon (small winery; scarce)

✔ **Burgess Cellars:** Zinfandel, Cabernet Sauvignon

✔ **Cain Cellars:** Cain Five (five Bordeaux varieties), Cain Cuvée

✔ **Cakebread Cellars:** Cabernet Sauvignon, Sauvignon Blanc, Chardonnay

✔ **Caymus Vineyard:** Cabernet Sauvignon (especially *Special Selection*)

✔ **Chappellet:** Chenin Blanc, Cabernet Sauvignon

✔ **Charles Krug:** Cabernet Sauvignon, Chardonnay (Family Reserves)

✔ **Chateau Montelena:** Cabernet Sauvignon, Calistoga Cuvée Red, Chardonnay

✔ **Clos du Val:** Cabernet Sauvignon, Sémillon, Chardonnay

✔ **Corison:** Cabernet Sauvignon

✔ **Cuvaison:** Chardonnay, Cabernet Sauvignon

✔ **Dalla Valle:** Cabernet Sauvignon, Maya (blend of Cabernet Franc/Cabernet Sauvignon)

✔ **Diamond Creek:** Cabernet Sauvignon

✔ **Dominus Estate:** Dominus (mainly Cabernet Sauvignon), Napanook

✔ **Duckhorn:** Merlot, Cabernet Sauvignon, Sauvignon Blanc

✔ **Dunn Vineyards:** Cabernet Sauvignon (especially Howell Mountain)

✔ **Far Niente:** Cabernet Sauvignon, Chardonnay

✔ **Fife Vineyards:** Zinfandel, Cabernet Sauvignon, Petite Sirah

- **Flora Springs:** Trilogy (blend of Cabernet Sauvignon, Merlot, Cabernet Franc), Cabernet Sauvignon Reserve, Soliloquy (Sauvignon Blanc)

- **Forman Vineyard:** Chardonnay, Cabernet Sauvignon

- **Franciscan Estate:** Chardonnay, Magnificat Red, Cabernet Sauvignon

- **Franus Winery:** Zinfandel, Cabernet Sauvignon

- **Freemark Abbey:** Cabernet Sauvignon (Bosché and Sycamore Vineyards)

- **Frog's Leap Winery:** Cabernet Sauvignon, Zinfandel, Sauvignon Blanc

- **Grace Family Vineyards:** Cabernet Sauvignon (small production; mailing list only)

- **Grgich Hills Cellar:** Chardonnay, Cabernet Sauvignon, Zinfandel, Fumé Blanc

- **Groth Vineyards:** Cabernet Sauvignon (especially Reserve)

- **Harlan Estate:** Cabernet Sauvignon (small winery; very scarce)

- **Heitz Wine Cellars:** Cabernet Sauvignon (Martha's Vineyard)

- **Hendry Ranch:** Zinfandel (all single-vineyard wines)

- **Hess Collection Winery:** Cabernet Sauvignon, Chardonnay

- **Lang & Reed:** Cabernet Franc

- **Long Vineyards:** Chardonnay, Riesling, Pinot Grigio

- **Markham Vineyards:** Chardonnay, Merlot, Cabernet Sauvignon

- **Mayacamas Vineyards:** Cabernet Sauvignon, Sauvignon Blanc

- **Mount Veeder Winery:** Cabernet Sauvignon, Reserve Red

- **Newton Vineyard:** Chardonnay, Merlot, Cabernet Sauvignon

- **Nickel & Nickel:** Cabernet Sauvignon (all single-vineyard wines)

- **Opus One:** Opus One (mainly Cabernet Sauvignon)

- **Pahlmeyer Winery:** Red (Cabernet blend), Merlot, Chardonnay

- **Patz & Hall:** Chardonnay

- **Joseph Phelps Vineyards:** Insignia (Cabernet blend), Cabernet Sauvignon

- **Pine Ridge Winery:** Cabernet Sauvignon, Chardonnay

- **Quintessa Estate:** Quintessa (Bordeaux blend)

- **Robert Mondavi:** Cabernet Sauvignon Reserve, Pinot Noir Reserve

- **Rubicon Estate (formerly Niebaum-Coppola):** Rubicon (mainly Cabernet Sauvignon), Edizone Pennino Zinfandel

- **Rudd Estate:** Chardonnay, Sauvignon Blanc, Cabernet Sauvignon

- **Saddleback Cellars:** Cabernet Sauvignon

- **Saintsbury:** Pinot Noir (all), Chardonnay

- **Selene:** Merlot, Sauvignon Blanc

- **Shafer Vineyards:** Cabernet Sauvignon, Merlot

- **Silver Oak Cellars:** Cabernet Sauvignon

- **Silverado Vineyards:** Cabernet Sauvignon, Chardonnay (Carneros)

- **Smith-Madrone:** Riesling, Chardonnay, Cabernet Sauvignon

- ✔ **Spottswoode Winery:** Cabernet Sauvignon, Sauvignon Blanc

- ✔ **Staglin Family Vineyard:** Cabernet Sauvignon

- ✔ **Stag's Leap Wine Cellars:** Cask 23 (Cabernet blend), Cabernet Sauvignon (Fay Vineyard and SLV), Chardonnay

- ✔ **Stony Hill Vineyard:** Chardonnay, Riesling

- ✔ **Storybook Mountain:** Zinfandel

- ✔ **Swanson Vineyards:** Cabernet Sauvignon, Merlot, Syrah

- ✔ **Trefethen Vineyards:** Cabernet Sauvignon, Chardonnay, Riesling (dry)

- ✔ **Turley Wine Cellars:** Zinfandel (all single-vineyard Zinfandels)

- ✔ **Turnbull Cellars:** Cabernet Sauvignon, Turnbull Red "Black Label"

- ✔ **Viader Vineyards:** Viader Red (Cabernet Sauvignon/Cabernet Franc)

- ✔ **ZD Wines:** Cabernet Sauvignon, Chardonnay

Down to Earth in Sonoma

If you leave San Francisco over the beautiful Golden Gate Bridge, you'll be in Sonoma in an hour. The differences between Napa and Sonoma are remarkable. Many of Napa's wineries are showy (even downright luxurious), but most of Sonoma's are rustic, country-like, and laid-back. The millionaires bought into Napa; Sonoma is just folks (with some exceptions, of course).

On the other hand, the famously successful Gallo is also in Sonoma, and so are Sebastiani, Glen Ellen, Korbel, Kendall-Jackson, Simi, and Jordan wineries — not exactly small-time operations! We have the sneaking suspicion that if we visit Sonoma in ten years, it'll bear a striking resemblance to Napa. But we hope not — we like it just the way it is.

Sonoma's viticultural areas

Sonoma is more than twice as large as Napa, it's more spread out, and it has almost as many wineries — more than 200. Its climate is similar to Napa's, except that some areas near the coast are definitely cooler. Although there's plenty of Chardonnay, Cabernet Sauvignon, and Merlot in Sonoma, the region's varied microclimates and terrain have allowed three other varieties — Pinot Noir, Zinfandel, and Sauvignon Blanc — to excel.

Following are the AVAs of Sonoma County, listed roughly from south to north with their principal grape varieties and wines:

- ✔ **Los Carneros (part in Napa Valley):** Pinot Noir, Chardonnay, sparkling wine, and Merlot

- ✔ **Sonoma Valley:** Chardonnay (to a lesser extent, Pinot Noir, Cabernet Sauvignon, Zinfandel)

- ✔ **Sonoma Mountain:** Cabernet Sauvignon

- ✔ **Bennett Valley:** Chardonnay, Sauvignon Blanc, Merlot

- ✔ **Russian River Valley:** Pinot Noir, Chardonnay, sparkling wine, Zinfandel

- ✔ **Sonoma-Green Valley (within Russian River Valley):** Sparkling wine, Chardonnay, Pinot Noir

- ✔ **Chalk Hill (within Russian River Valley):** Chardonnay, Sauvignon Blanc

- ✔ **Dry Creek Valley:** Zinfandel, Cabernet Sauvignon

- ✔ **Alexander Valley:** Cabernet Sauvignon, Chardonnay, Sauvignon Blanc

> ✔ **Knight's Valley:** Cabernet Sauvignon, Sauvignon Blanc

> ✔ **Rockpile (in the northwestern part of the county):** Zinfandel, Cabernet Sauvignon, Syrah, Petite Sirah

Sonoma County has two more AVAs: Northern Sonoma, a patchwork area encompassing Russian River Valley, Alexander Valley, Dry Creek Valley, and Knight's Valley; and Sonoma Coast, a hodgepodge of land in western Sonoma, along the coast. Also, the North Coast AVA takes in Sonoma County.

Pinot Noir lovers should look for wines from Russian River Valley producers, such as Williams & Selyem, Rochioli, Gary Farrell, Lynmar, and Dehlinger. We agree with those who say that the Russian River Valley is the source of some of the best Pinot Noir in the entire New World.

Sonoma producers and wines

The following list of recommended producers includes some of Sonoma's better wineries, listed alphabetically, along with their best wines. It's *slightly* less staggering than the Napa list.

Although all these wineries are in Sonoma County, some of their wines are made from grapes grown elsewhere. Cline Cellars, for example, uses grapes from Contra Costa County, east of San Francisco. Check the labels to find out.

> ✔ **Arrowood Vineyards:** Chardonnay, Cabernet Sauvignon, Syrah

> ✔ **Benziger Family Winery:** Cabernet Sauvignon, Sauvignon Blanc

- ✔ **B. R. Cohn:** Cabernet Sauvignon (Olive Hill Vineyard)

- ✔ **Chalk Hill Estate:** Sauvignon Blanc, Chardonnay, Cabernet Sauvignon

- ✔ **Chateau Souverain:** Cabernet Sauvignon, Sauvignon Blanc

- ✔ **Chateau St. Jean:** Chardonnay (Robert Young, Belle Terre Vineyards), Cabernet Sauvignon (Cinq Cépages)

- ✔ **Cline Cellars:** Mourvèdre, Zinfandel

- ✔ **Clos du Bois:** Marlstone (Cabernet blend), Chardonnay

- ✔ **Dehlinger Winery:** Pinot Noir, Chardonnay, Syrah

- ✔ **Dry Creek Vineyard:** Fumé Blanc, Chenin Blanc, Zinfandel

- ✔ **Ferrari-Carano:** Chardonnay, Fumé Blanc, Cabernet Sauvignon

- ✔ **Fisher Vineyards:** Chardonnay, Cabernet Sauvignon

- ✔ **Flowers Vineyard & Winery:** Pinot Noir, Chardonnay

- ✔ **Foppiano Vineyards:** Petite Sirah, Cabernet Sauvignon, Merlot

- ✔ **Gallo Family Vineyards:** Chardonnay (Laguna Ranch), Zinfandel (Frei Ranch)

- ✔ **Gary Farrell Wines:** Pinot Noir, Chardonnay, Zinfandel

- ✔ **Geyser Peak Winery:** Chardonnay, Cabernet Sauvignon

- ✔ **Hanna Winery:** Sauvignon Blanc, Zinfandel, Cabernet Sauvignon

✔ **Hanzell Vineyards:** Chardonnay

✔ **Hartford Court:** Pinot Noir (all), Zinfandel

✔ **Jordan Vineyard:** Cabernet Sauvignon, Chardonnay

✔ **Kendall-Jackson:** Cabernet Sauvignon, Chardonnay, Zinfandel

✔ **Kenwood Vineyards:** Cabernet Sauvignon (Artist Series), Zinfandel

✔ **Kistler Vineyards:** Chardonnay, Pinot Noir

✔ **Joseph Swan Vineyards:** Pinot Noir, Zinfandel

✔ **La Crema Winery:** Chardonnay, Pinot Noir

✔ **Laurel Glen Vineyard:** Cabernet Sauvignon, Reds, Terra Rosa

✔ **Lynmar Winery:** Pinot Noir, Chardonnay

✔ **Marcassin:** Chardonnay (all vineyards; very scarce, by mailing list)

✔ **Marietta Cellars:** Petite Sirah, Zinfandel, Old Vine Red (Zin blend)

✔ **Marimar Torres Estate:** Chardonnay, Pinot Noir

✔ **Martin Ray Winery:** Cabernet Sauvignon, Merlot, Chardonnay

✔ **Martinelli Vineyard:** Zinfandel, Chardonnay (Russian River Valley)

✔ **Matanzas Creek Winery:** Chardonnay, Sauvignon Blanc, Merlot

✔ **Paul Hobbs:** Cabernet Sauvignon, Chardonnay, Pinot Noir

✔ **Peter Michael Winery:** Chardonnay, Les Pavots (Cabernet blend)

✔ **Preston of Dry Creek:** Zinfandel, Syrah, Barbera

✔ **Quivira Vineyards:** Zinfandel, Syrah, Petite Sirah

- ✔ **A. Rafanelli Winery:** Zinfandel, Cabernet Sauvignon (mailing list)

- ✔ **Ravenswood:** Zinfandel (single-vineyards), Merlot (Sangiacomo Vineyard), Pickberry (Cabernet Sauvignon/Merlot blend)

- ✔ **J. Rochioli Vineyard:** Pinot Noir (all), Sauvignon Blanc, Zinfandel

- ✔ **Saint Francis Winery:** Zinfandel, Merlot, Cabernet Sauvignon

- ✔ **Sausal Winery:** Zinfandel (all), Sangiovese

- ✔ **Sebastiani Vineyards:** Cabernet Sauvignon, Merlot, Chardonnay

- ✔ **Seghesio Family Estates:** Zinfandel (all), Sangiovese, Barbera

- ✔ **Sonoma-Cutrer Vineyards:** Chardonnay (all selections)

- ✔ **Stonestreet:** Cabernet Sauvignon (all), Chardonnay, Sauvignon Blanc

- ✔ **Trentadue Winery:** Petite Sirah, Old Patch Red

- ✔ **Williams Selyem Winery:** Pinot Noir (all), Zinfandel, Chardonnay (all wines very scarce; sold by mailing list)

Mendocino and Lake Counties

Lake County, dominated by Clear Lake, is Napa's neighbor to the north, and Mendocino County is directly north of Sonoma. If you have the chance, it's worth your while to drive up the beautiful California coastline from San Francisco on Route 1 to the quaint, old town of Mendocino — perhaps with a side trip to view the magnificent, giant redwoods of the Pacific Coast. Tourists are scarcer up here than in Napa or

Sonoma, and that makes it all the nicer: You'll be genuinely welcomed at the wineries.

The cool Anderson Valley in Mendocino County is ideal for growing Chardonnay, Pinot Noir, Gewürztraminer, and Riesling, and for the production of sparkling wine. The wily Louis Roederer Champagne house bypassed Napa and Sonoma to start its sparkling wine operation here and has done extremely well in a short time — as have Scharffenberger and Handley, two other successful sparkling wine producers in Anderson Valley.

The following alphabetical lists include recommended producers and their best wines. Here are our picks for Mendocino County:

- **Edmeades:** Zinfandel (especially single-vineyards)

- **Fetzer Vineyards:** Pinot Noir Reserve, Cabernet Sauvignon Reserve

- **Greenwood Ridge Vineyards:** Riesling, Pinot Noir, Zinfandel

- **Handley Cellars:** Chardonnay, Gewürztraminer, Sauvignon Blanc

- **Lazy Creek Vineyards:** Gewürztraminer, Riesling

- **Lolonis Winery:** Cabernet Sauvignon (all), Zinfandel

- **McDowell Valley Vineyards:** Syrah, Viognier

- **Navarro Vineyards:** Gewürztraminer, Chardonnay (Reserve)

And here are the producers we recommend in Lake County:

- **Guenoc Winery:** Cabernet Sauvignon, Chardonnay, Langtry Meritage Red (Cabernet blend), Petite Sirah Reserve

> ✔ **Steele Wines:** Chardonnay, Zinfandel, Pinot
> Noir, Pinot Blanc
>
> ✔ **Wildhurst Vineyards:** Cabernet Sauvignon,
> Chardonnay, Merlot

Thar's Wine in Them Thar (Sierra) Foothills

No wine region in America has a more romantic past than the Sierra Foothills. The Gold Rush of 1849 carved a place in history for the foothills of the Sierra Nevada Mountains. It also brought vineyards to the area to provide wine for the thirsty miners. One of the vines planted at that time was certainly Zinfandel — still the region's most famous wine. Many of the oldest grapevines in the United States, some over 100 years old — mainly Zinfandel — are here in the Sierra Foothills.

The Sierra Foothills is a sprawling wine region east of Sacramento, centered in Amador and El Dorado Counties, but spreading north and south of both. Two of its best-known AVAs are the Shenandoah Valley and Fiddletown. Summers can be hot, but many vineyards are situated as high as 1,500 feet — such as around Placerville in El Dorado — and evenings are very cool. Soil throughout the region is mainly volcanic in origin.

Following are our recommended producers in the Sierra Foothills (listed alphabetically), along with their best wines:

> ✔ **Amador Foothill Winery:** Zinfandel
>
> ✔ **Boeger Winery:** Zinfandel, Barbera, Sauvignon
> Blanc

- ✔ **Karly:** Zinfandel, Syrah, Sauvignon Blanc, Marsanne

- ✔ **Lava Cap Winery:** Barbera, Cabernet Sauvignon, Petite Sirah

- ✔ **Monteviña:** Zinfandel, Syrah

- ✔ **Renaissance Vineyard:** Cabernet Sauvignon, Riesling (Late Harvest), Sauvignon Blanc

- ✔ **Renwood Winery:** Barbera, Zinfandel (especially Grandpère Vineyard)

- ✔ **Shenandoah Vineyards:** Zinfandel, Sauvignon Blanc

- ✔ **Sierra Vista Winery:** Zinfandel, Syrah

- ✔ **Sobon Estate:** Zinfandel, Viognier

- ✔ **Stevenot Winery:** Syrah, Tempranillo, Zinfandel

San Francisco Bay Area

The San Francisco Bay Area includes wine regions north, east, and south of the city: Marin County to the north; Alameda County and Livermore Valley to the east; and Santa Clara Valley and San Mateo County to the south.

The urban spread east and south of San Francisco, from the cities of Palo Alto to San Jose (Silicon Valley) and eastward, has taken its toll on vineyards in the Livermore and Santa Clara valleys. These two growing regions, both cooled by breezes from the San Francisco Bay, are now relatively small.

In Livermore, directly east of San Francisco, Sauvignon Blanc and Sémillon have always done well. In Santa Clara Valley, south of San Francisco with the Santa Cruz Mountains on its western side, Chardonnay, Cabernet Sauvignon, and Merlot are the three big grape varieties (and wines).

We list our recommended wineries alphabetically, by
locality:

✔ **Marin County:**

- **Kalin Cellars:** Sauvignon Blanc, Sémillon,
  Chardonnay, Pinot Noir; grapes from diverse
  areas, including Livermore

- **Sean H. Thackrey:** Orion Old Vines Red
  (Syrah blend), Sirius (Petite Sirah); grapes
  from several different areas, including Napa

✔ **Alameda County:**

- **Edmunds St. John:** Syrah, Rocks and Gravel
  (Rhône blend); grapes are sourced from
  throughout the state

- **Rosenblum Cellars:** Zinfandel (especially
  single-vineyards); uses mainly Sonoma Valley
  and Napa Valley fruit

✔ **Livermore Valley:**

- **Concannon Vineyard:** Chardonnay,
  Petite Sirah

- **Murrietta's Well:** Zinfandel, Red Meritage
  (Cabernet blend)

- **Wente Family Estates:** Chardonnay,
  Sauvignon Blanc

✔ **Santa Clara Valley (other than Santa Cruz
Mountains):**

- **J. Lohr Winery:** Chardonnay, Cabernet
  Sauvignon (Paso Robles)

✔ **San Mateo County:**

- **Cronin Vineyards:** Chardonnay (all selections)

- **Thomas Fogarty Winery:** Gewürztraminer,
  Chardonnay, Pinot Noir

Santa Cruz Mountains

Standing atop one of the isolated Santa Cruz Mountains, you can quickly forget that you're only an hour's drive south of San Francisco. The rugged, wild beauty of this area has attracted quite a few winemakers, including some of the best in the state. (Paul Draper of Ridge Vineyards and Randall Grahm of Bonny Doon are but two.) The climate is cool on the ocean side, where Pinot Noir thrives. On the San Francisco Bay side, Cabernet Sauvignon is the important red variety. Chardonnay is a leading variety on both sides.

We list our recommended Santa Cruz Mountains wine producers alphabetically, along with their best wines:

- **Bargetto:** Chardonnay, Cabernet Sauvignon, Merlot

- **Bonny Doon Vineyard:** Le Cigare Volant Red (Rhône blend), Old Telegram (Mourvèdre)

- **David Bruce Winery:** Pinot Noir (Santa Cruz), Zinfandel (Paso Robles)

- **Cinnabar Vineyards:** Chardonnay, Cabernet Sauvignon

- **Kathryn Kennedy Winery:** Cabernet Sauvignon, Syrah

- **Mount Eden Vineyards:** Chardonnay Estate, Cabernet Sauvignon Estate, Pinot Noir Estate

- **Ridge Vineyards:** Cabernet Sauvignon Monte Bello, Geyserville (Zin blend), Zinfandel (all)

- **Santa Cruz Mountain Vineyard:** Pinot Noir, Cabernet Sauvignon

What's New in Old Monterey

Monterey County has a little bit of everything — a
beautiful coastline, the chic town of Carmel, some
very cool (as in temperature, not chicness) vineyard
districts and some very warm areas, mountain wineries and Salinas Valley wineries, a few gigantic wine
firms and lots of small ones. Like most California wine
regions, Monterey has been changing rapidly during
the past two decades, and now seven official AVAs
exist here, covering about 75 wineries:

- ✔ Arroyo Seco
- ✔ Carmel Valley
- ✔ Chalone
- ✔ Hames Valley
- ✔ Monterey
- ✔ San Luca
- ✔ Santa Lucia Highlands

Chardonnay is the leading varietal wine in Monterey
County — as it is in most of the state. But the cooler
parts of Monterey are also principal sources of
Riesling and Gewürztraminer. Cabernet Sauvignon,
and Pinot Noir are the leading red varieties in the
mountain areas.

Here are our recommended producers in Monterey
County, listed alphabetically, along with one producer from neighboring San Benito County:

- ✔ **Bernardus Winery:** Chardonnay, Sauvignon
  Blanc, Marinus (mainly Cabernet Sauvignon),
  Pinot Noir
- ✔ **Calera** (San Benito County): Pinot Noir (espe-
  cially single-vineyard selections), Viognier,
  Chardonnay

- ✔ **Chalone Vineyard:** Chardonnay, Pinot Blanc, Pinot Noir

- ✔ **Chateau Julien:** Chardonnay, Merlot, Cabernet Sauvignon

- ✔ **Estancia Estates:** Chardonnay, Cabernet Sauvignon, Merlot, Pinot Noir

- ✔ **Morgan Winery:** Chardonnay, Pinot Noir, Pinot Gris, Syrah

- ✔ **Paraiso Vineyards:** Pinot Noir, Chardonnay, Riesling, Syrah

- ✔ **Robert Talbott Vineyards:** Chardonnay

Contrasts in San Luis Obispo

San Luis Obispo County is an area of vastly diverse AVAs, including the warm, hilly Paso Robles region (north of the town of San Luis Obispo), where Zinfandel and Cabernet Sauvignon reign, and the cool, coastal Edna Valley and Arroyo Grande (south of the town), home of some very good Pinot Noirs and Chardonnays.

Paso Robles, with more than 90 wineries, is in the heart of California's Central Coast, about equidistant from San Francisco and Los Angeles. Its wines are so different from those of the two coastal areas that we name the producers separately. We recommend the following producers in San Luis Obispo County (listed alphabetically, along with their best wines):

- ✔ **Paso Robles:**

  - **Adelaida Cellars:** Pinot Noir, Zinfandel, Cabernet Sauvignon

  - **Eberle Winery:** Zinfandel, Cabernet Sauvignon, Viognier

- **EOS Estate Winery:** Zinfandel, Cabernet Sauvignon, Petite Sirah
- **Justin Vineyards:** Isosceles (Cabernet blend), Cabernet Sauvignon, Cabernet Franc, Chardonnay
- **Meridian Vineyards** (also has vineyards in Edna Valley and Santa Barbara): Chardonnay (especially Reserve), Syrah
- **Peachy Canyon Winery:** Zinfandel
- **Rabbit Ridge Vineyards:** Zinfandel, Primitivo, Syrah, Pinot Grigio
- **Tablas Creek Vineyard:** Mourvèdre, Grenache, Syrah, Roussanne
- **Treana Winery:** Red (mainly Cabernet Sauvignon, Merlot, Syrah), White (mainly Marsanne and Viognier)
- **Wild Horse Winery:** Pinot Noir, Merlot, Cabernet Sauvignon

✔ **Edna Valley and Arroyo Grande:**

- **Alban Vineyards:** Viognier (Estate) Roussanne, Syrah, Grenache
- **Claiborne & Churchill:** Riesling, Pinot Gris, Pinot Noir
- **Edna Valley Vineyard:** Chardonnay, Pinot Noir, Cabernet Sauvignon
- **Laetitia Vineyard:** Chardonnay, Pinot Noir
- **Saucelito Canyon Vineyard:** Zinfandel
- **Talley Vineyards:** Chardonnay, Pinot Noir

Santa Barbara, California Paradise

The most exciting AVAs in California — if not in the entire United States — are in Santa Barbara County. Even though Spanish missionaries planted vineyards there 200 years ago, it wasn't until 1975 that the first major winery (Firestone Vineyards) opened. In light of what we now know — that is, how well-suited Santa Barbara is to grape growing — 1975 was a late start.

The cool Santa Maria, Santa Ynez, and Los Alamos valleys — which lie north of the city of Santa Barbara — run east to west, opening toward the Pacific Ocean and channeling in the ocean air. The cool climate is ideal for Pinot Noir and Chardonnay. In the Santa Maria Valley, one of the main sources of these varieties, the average temperature during the growing season is a mere 74°F. Farther south, in the Santa Ynez Valley, Riesling also does well.

Santa Barbara is generally recognized as one of the six great American wine regions for Pinot Noir. In Santa Barbara, Pinot Noir wines seem to burst with luscious strawberry fruit, laced with herbal tones. These wines tend to be precocious; they're delicious in their first four or five years.

Here are some recommended producers in Santa Barbara (listed alphabetically) and their best wines:

- **Alma Rosa:** Chardonnay, Pinot Gris, Pinot Noir
- **Au Bon Climat:** Pinot Noir, Chardonnay (especially single-vineyard bottlings of both), Pinot Gris/Pinot Blanc
- **Babcock Vineyards:** Sauvignon Blanc, Chardonnay, Pinot Noir

✔ **The Brander Vineyard:** Sauvignon Blanc

✔ **Byron Vineyard:** Chardonnay (especially Nielson Vineyard), Pinot Noir

✔ **Cambria Winery:** Chardonnay, Pinot Noir (Julia's Vineyard), Syrah

✔ **Cottonwood Canyon:** Pinot Noir

✔ **Daniel Gehrs:** Chenin Blanc, Dry Riesling, Gewürztraminer, Syrah

✔ **Fess Parker Winery:** Chardonnay, Syrah, Pinot Noir

✔ **Fiddlehead Cellars:** Pinot Noir, Sauvignon Blanc

✔ **Firestone Vineyard:** Chardonnay, Sauvignon Blanc

✔ **Foley Estate:** Chardonnay, Pinot Noir

✔ **Foxen Vineyard:** Pinot Noir, Syrah, Viognier, Chenin Blanc

✔ **Gainey Vineyard:** Chardonnay, Pinot Noir, Sauvignon Blanc

✔ **Hitching Post:** Pinot Noir, Syrah

✔ **IO Wines:** IO (Rhône blend, Syrah/Grenache/ Mourvèdre), Syrah

✔ **Lane Tanner:** Pinot Noir, Syrah

✔ **Lincourt Vineyards:** Pinot Noir, Syrah, Chardonnay

✔ **Longoria Wines:** Chardonnay, Pinot Noir, Cabernet Franc, Syrah

✔ **The Ojai Vineyard:** Pinot Noir, Syrah, Chardonnay

✔ **Qupé Cellars:** Syrah, Chardonnay, Roussanne, Marsanne, Viognier

- ✔ **Sanford Winery:** Pinot Noir (especially Sanford & Benedict Vineyard), Chardonnay, Sauvignon Blanc

- ✔ **Santa Barbara Winery:** Pinot Noir, Chardonnay, Syrah

- ✔ **Zaca Mesa Winery:** Syrah, Rousanne, Chardonnay

Chapter 3

Becoming a French Wine Connoisseur

. . . .

In This Chapter
▶ Seeing how land and wine are connected in France
▶ Finding out about the three Bs of French wine
▶ Discovering why Champagne is in a class by itself

. . . .

*S*ome people are born with certain talents, and some countries are born with certain gifts. In the case of France, the ability to grow wine grapes and make good wine is hard-wired into the land and the people who live there. That's why France is not only the greatest wine-producing country on Earth but also the greatest wine culture.

France has been the leader of the winemaking world for centuries. France is number one not only in wine production (in many years) but also in wine consumption. In the quality department, the most critically acclaimed, most treasured red wines, white wines, sparkling wines, *and* sweet wines all come from France. The country's renown is such that winemakers from all over the world find inspiration and motivation in French wines.

A Perfect Pair: France and Wine

France is large by European standards — it's the largest country in western Europe — but compared to countries such as the United States or Australia, it isn't really such a big place. (All of France could fit easily into Texas, for example, with plenty of room to spare.) And yet, France has a strong diversity of soil types and climates. Each of France's major wine regions has different growing conditions for its grapes. (Figure 3-1 depicts France's wine regions.)

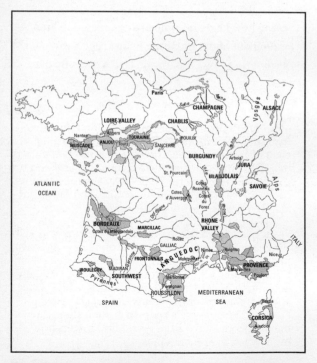

Figure 3-1: France's wine regions.

Natural talents

France's thousands of years of winemaking experience count for a lot. But the fact is, France had a couple other things going for her since Day One: climates extremely suitable for growing high-quality wine grapes and the right types of soils in the right climates.

Climate ups and downs

France has ideal climates for growing wine grapes thanks to where the country happens to be situated relative to the rest of Europe, and thanks to the lay of the land within France's borders. The following different climates each favor the cultivation of different grape varieties and the production of different types of wine:

- ✔ Water surrounds France on three sides: the Atlantic Ocean on the west, the English Channel on the north, and the Mediterranean Sea along part of the country's southern border. These bodies of water influence the climate of the land nearby. In particular, winds passing over the Atlantic's Gulf Stream carry moisture and warm air to western France, providing a climate that's more suitable for grape growing than France's northerly position might suggest.

- ✔ The Massif Central, a high plateau in south central France, blocks the Atlantic's maritime influence about halfway across the country — and creates a particular climate in eastern France (hot but relatively short summers, and cold winters) that's distinctly different from the damp, temperate climate in the west. Farther east, France is landlocked and mountainous, with the mighty Alps Mountains separating France from Italy and Switzerland.

> ✔ The Mediterranean Sea creates yet another climate pattern in southern France: warm, dry, long summers and mild, rainy winters.

Old dirt

The variation in soil types within France has to do with the geological origins of the European continent — the melting of polar ice caps, the drying of seas, the decomposition of rocks, and so forth. Different wine regions of France have markedly different soils. For example:

> ✔ Gravel is found in the western part of Bordeaux
>
> ✔ Chalky soil exists in Champagne, in the northeast
>
> ✔ Granite is found in Beaujolais, in the southeast
>
> ✔ Large stones exist in the Châteauneuf-du-Pape district of the southern Rhône Valley

Even within individual wine regions, the soil varies quite a lot. The difference between western Bordeaux and eastern Bordeaux is one classic example: Different soils in each area favor different grape varieties. Within the region of Alsace, the soils change literally from one hillside to the next, and within Burgundy, soils change between vineyards separated from each other by the width of a cow path.

What's important about France's soils is that they're the right soils in the right climates for the right grape varieties. Where the climate is rainy (as in Bordeaux), for example, the soil provides good drainage. Where there's an impressionable grape variety, such as Pinot Noir, the soil varies from patch to patch (as in Burgundy) to create compellingly individual wines.

French wine-think

The French attribute every nuance in a wine to the particular place where the grapes grow — to the rain that falls or refrains from falling; the sun that shines down on the vineyard; the wind that warms or cools the air; and the soil that holds the rain or drains it, that reflects the sun's heat back onto the grapes, or contains just the right minerals.

The French have a single word for the whole package of natural, interactive forces that affect the grapevine and its fruit: *terroir* (pronounced *ter wahr*). *Terroir* encompasses

- ✔ The soil and subsoil of a vineyard, including its mineral content, fertility, and drainage
- ✔ How the vineyard is situated, on a slope, for example, or near a river
- ✔ The climate of the wine region, including sun, heat, wind, rain, and humidity
- ✔ The grape variety or varieties that grow in the vineyard

Every wine comes from a unique *terroir,* and — in the Gallic way of looking at wine — is what it is because of its *terroir.*

The concept of *terroir* is so fundamental to French wine that it even dictates how the wines are named: The overwhelming majority of French wines carry the name of the place where the grapes grow because the place (rather than just the grape variety) is what makes the wines the way they are. Depending on the wine, the place might be any of the following:

- ✔ A large wine region
- ✔ A district within a region
- ✔ A single vineyard

A note on names

If a wine comes from a classic region, the label will carry the words "*Appellation . . . Contrôlée*" (*ahp pel laht zee ohn con troh lay*) in small print under the name of the wine. Between the two words is the name of the place that's the wine official name.

Appellation Contrôlée translates as "regulated name." Sometimes in reading about French wines, you might see the phrase *Appellation d'Origine Contrôlée*; it translates as "regulated place name." The two phrases are used interchangeably and mean the same thing. People who talk about French wine a lot use the abbreviations "AC" or "AOC" for these phrases.

The Elite Red Wines of Bordeaux

The Bordeaux wine region (pictured in Figure 3-1) lies in the southern part of western France, on the Atlantic Coast. Bordeaux's reputation as a great wine region rests on its most superb reds, legendary and long-lived wines made by historic wine estates (called *châteaux*), which can improve for several decades. Seventy-five to 80 percent of Bordeaux's wines are red. (Most of the rest is dry white, and 2 or 3 percent is stunning dessert wine.)

Red Bordeaux is always a blended wine. It's made from two to five so-called *black* grape varieties. The percentage of each grape variety used in a particular red Bordeaux wine can change from year to year, depending on the climate and how each variety has fared during the growing season. The percentage also varies from one estate to another.

The five grape varieties of red Bordeaux are as follows:

- ✔ Cabernet Sauvignon (*cab er nay so vee n'yohn*)
- ✔ Merlot (*mer loh*)
- ✔ Cabernet Franc (*cab er nay frahn*)
- ✔ Petit Verdot (*peh tee vair doe*)
- ✔ Malbec (*mahl bec*)

Either Cabernet Sauvignon or Merlot is the dominant variety in practically all red Bordeaux wines; Cabernet Franc is the third most-utilized variety, followed by Petite Verdot and Malbec.

The lay of the Bordeaux lands

The Bordeaux region is quite large, encompassing more than a quarter of a million acres of vineyards, and it produces about 660 million bottles annually (about 10 percent of France's wine, but more than 25 percent of its AOC wine). Naturally, climate and soil vary across this large area. Four major districts, each with its own particular *terroir,* exist within the region:

- ✔ Haut-Médoc (*oh meh dock*)
- ✔ Graves/Pessac-Léognan (*grahv/peh sack lay oh nyahn*)
- ✔ St.-Emilion (*sant em eel yon*)
- ✔ Pomerol (*pohm eh roll*)

Wines with the Haut-Médoc, St.-Emilion, or Pomerol appellations must be red; Graves or Pessac-Léognan wines may be red or white.

Because of certain similarities in the wines, and for historical reasons, these four major districts for red Bordeaux are often grouped as two entities, which are often known as the *Left Bank* and the *Right Bank*. The Médoc peninsula and Graves/Pessac-Léognan make up the Left Bank; St.-Emilion and Pomerol are Right Bank districts.

The Left Bank style

Our very favorite red Bordeaux wines come from the Left Bank of Bordeaux, especially from the Haut-Médoc and Pessac-Léognan districts. Generally speaking, the red Bordeaux wines from the Left Bank are quite tannic and austere when they're young (see Chapter 1 for the scoop on tannins), and they have a pronounced black currant aroma and flavor. With age, they develop complex secondary aromas and flavors, such as stewed fruit, leather, earth, and tobacco; their colors lighten and flavors soften as the tannin begins to drop out of the wine.

These wines need ten years or more to come into their own, and the best of them are capable of developing further for decades. The most common mistake regarding Left Bank Bordeaux wines is drinking them when they're less than ten years old: They can taste harsh and bitter at this age, and then you wonder what all the fuss is about red Bordeaux.

The Right Bank style

The Right Bank, with its two major subregions of St.-Emilion and Pomerol, has soil that's perfect for the Merlot grape variety — the Right Bank's dominant grape variety. Cabernet Franc, which ripens faster than Cabernet Sauvignon, is the second-most important variety on the Right Bank.

The 1855 Classification

No classification of Bordeaux wines has created more of an impact than the "1855 Classification of the Great Growths of the Gironde." Here's how this legendary classification came about.

The 1855 Exposition in Paris was going to have a special guest — Queen Victoria of England. Since the Brits had always been partial to Bordeaux (and, in fact, owned this region at one time, then called Aquitaine), the organizers of the Exposition asked the Bordeaux Chamber of Commerce to develop the ultimate classification of great Bordeaux wines. The Chamber of Commerce in turn asked the *négociants* of Bordeaux — the merchants who bought and sold Bordeaux wine — to devise the list. The *négociants* based their classification on the prices that the wines commanded at that time, as well as the wines' track records over the past 100 years, and came up with a ranked list of 61 red Bordeaux wines.

These 61 wines became known as "Classified Growths" or, in French, "*Grands Crus Classés*" wines (a *cru* in Bordeaux refers to a wine estate). At that time, the Haut-Médoc sub-region dominated the Bordeaux wine trade, and so 60 of the 61 wines were Haut-Médoc wines; one was from the Graves (the part now known as Pessac-Léognan). All of the Right Bank wines were shut out of the famous 1855 ranking.

Right Bank Bordeaux reds, such as St.-Emilions and Pomerols, are a good choice for the novice red Bordeaux drinker because they're less tannic and austere, and more approachable, than Left Bank Bordeaux. This difference is particularly noticeable when the wines are young (less than ten years old).

Although Right Bank red Bordeaux wines are readier to drink sooner than Left Bank Bordeaux, the better examples of these wines can live for many decades — nearly as long as Left Bank Bordeaux, especially in good vintages.

Bordeaux's best reds

In the following sections, we list some of the best red Bordeaux wines on the Left and Right Banks.

Great Haut-Médoc wines

Our favorite Haut-Médoc wines are all classified growths. We list them in our rough order of preference and include their village appellation after the wine.

- **Château Pichon-Longueville — Comtesse de Lalande** (Pauillac)
- **Château Ducru-Beaucaillou** (Saint-Julien)
- **Château Palmer** (Margaux)
- **Château Pichon-Longueville Baron** (Pauillac)
- **Château Gruaud-Larose** (St.-Julien)
- **Château Montrose** (St.-Estèphe)
- **Château Clerc-Milon** (Pauillac)
- **Château Grand-Puy-Lacoste** (Pauillac)
- **Château Léoville-Barton** (St.-Julien)
- **Château Lynch-Bages** (Pauillac)

Top Pessac-Léognan wines

Most of our favorite Pessac-Léognan wines are classified growths (in 1953 and 1959); only three of them are unclassified. We list them in our rough order of preference:

✔ Château La Mission-Haut-Brion

✔ Château Pape-Clément

✔ Château Malartic-Lagravière

✔ Château Smith-Haut-Lafitte

✔ Domaine de Chevalier

✔ Château Les Carmes Haut-Brion (unclassified)

✔ Château La Tour-Haut-Brion

✔ Château Larrivet–Haut-Brion (unclassified)

✔ Château La Louvière (unclassified)

✔ Château d'Olivier

The Best St.-Emilion Bordeaux

Without a doubt, the two greatest St.-Emilion wines are Château Cheval Blanc and Château Ausone. For additional recommendations, see the following list, which is in our rough order of preference. (Note that the official classification rank for each wine is listed in parentheses.)

✔ **Château Pavie** (Premier Grand Cru Classé)

✔ **Château Pavie-Macquin** (Grand Cru Classé)

✔ **Château Canon-La-Gaffelière** (Grand Cru Classé)

✔ **Château Pavie-Decesse** (Grand Cru Classé)

✔ **Château Troplong-Mondot** (Grand Cru Classé)

✔ **Château Beau-Séjour Bécot** (Premier Grand Cru Classé)

✔ **Château Monbousquet** (Grand Cru)

✔ **Château La Clusière** (Grand Cru Classé)

✔ **Clos de l'Oratoire** (Grand Cru Classé)

✔ **Château Figeac** (Premier Grand Cru Classé)

A Pomerol ranking (unofficial)

Even though the wines of the Pomerol subregion —
which, like St.-Emilion's, are all red — have never
been officially classified, we've come up with our own
ranking of these very wonderful wines. Here it is, in
our rough order of preference:

- ✔ Château Pétrus
- ✔ Château Lafleur
- ✔ Château Trotanoy
- ✔ Château L'Evangile
- ✔ Vieux-Château-Certan
- ✔ Château L'Eglise-Clinet
- ✔ Château Clinet
- ✔ Château La Fleur Pétrus
- ✔ Clos L'Eglise
- ✔ Château La Conseillante

Drinking red Bordeaux

We seldom order the best red Bordeaux wines in restaurants because the young wines from the currently
available vintages that dominate wine lists are far from
ready to drink. And when older vintages are available,
their prices are usually very expensive. The best restaurant strategy is to drink inexpensive, readier-to-
drink red Bordeaux — if it's available. Save the better,
mature red Bordeaux for drinking at home.

Red Bordeaux isn't the easiest wine to match
with food. It goes best with simple cuts of red
meat, lamb, or venison. It's also fine with hard
cheeses, such as Cheddar or Comté, and good,
crusty bread. (For advice on pairing wine with
food, see Chapter 5.)

A fine Bordeaux needs decanting, whether it's young or mature. A young wine will benefit from the extra aeration (at least an hour) that decanting provides. A mature (ten years or older) Bordeaux has sediment, a harmless but disagreeable byproduct, that's removed by careful decanting. Inexpensive Bordeaux wines don't need decanting.

Serve red Bordeaux at cool room temperatures — about 63°F to 66°F (18° to 19°C). A fine, large glass (not too wide) is best.

Burgundy, Master of Pinot Noir and Chardonnay

Burgundy is a long, narrow wine region in eastern France, southeast of Paris (refer to Figure 3-1). Nearly all the red wines of the Burgundy region derive from Pinot Noir. Pinot Noir is notorious throughout the wine world for being difficult to cultivate because it requires very specific soil and climate parameters to produce its best fruit — Burgundy has that climate and soil.

Chardonnay is the other important variety in the Burgundy region and the basis for the region's most important white wines. Although Chardonnay is a nearly universal variety today, it reaches its height in Burgundy, where it makes complex, masterful wines that can age for decades.

A complex wine region

Burgundy is a region of small vineyards, mixed ownership of vineyards, and relatively small production. Excluding the Beaujolais district, which we cover later in this chapter, Burgundy produces a total of about 22 million cases of wine annually. Burgundy's vineyards are also much smaller than Bordeaux's, meaning less wine is available from any one vineyard.

The limited scale of production in Burgundy has three repercussions:

✔ The wines are expensive.

✔ Multiple brands of any one wine are available.

✔ The name of a vineyard isn't a reliable indication of a wine's quality because every vineyard has several owners and winemakers, who vary in dedication and ability.

Burgundy's districts and the top producers in each

Four distinct districts make up the complex Burgundy wine region. From north to south, they are Chablis, Côte d'Or, Côte Chalonnaise, and Mâconnais.

Chablis, from Chablis, France

The Chablis district, the northernmost outpost of Burgundy, produces white wines only, 100 percent Chardonnay. In a good vintage, Chablis can be magical: pale straw in color with hints of green, turning light gold with age; bone dry and medium-bodied, with lively acidity that makes the wine great with seafood; concentrated in delicate, minerally aromas and an appley flavor that lingers long after you swallow.

Producers make Chablis in three different styles:

✔ Many use just stainless steel tanks, with absolutely no oak barrels at all — either in fermenting or aging the wine — in order to preserve the purest expression of Chablis's flavors. The producer Louis Michel is the greatest proponent of this style; other "no oak" producers include Jean-Marc Brocard, Long-Depaquit, A. Régnard, and Jean Durup.

✔ A few producers ferment or briefly age their wines in oak barrels, mainly used barrels that give less oaky flavor than new barrels. This style of Chablis is typically more full-bodied and can have some oaky aroma and flavor. Raveneau and René & Vincent Dauvissat are the leading producers of this style of Chablis.

✔ Quite a few producers are taking the middle ground, using no oak for their less-expensive Chablis and some oak aging for their more serious wines. These producers include Collet, Jean-Paul Droin, Jean Dauvissat, William Fèvre, and Domaine Laroche.

You can find good Chablis producers in all three styles. Our favorite Chablis producers, in our rough order of preference, are the following (the first three are virtually tied for first):

✔ François & Jean-Marie Raveneau

✔ René & Vincent Dauvissat

✔ Louis Michel & Fils

✔ Jean Collet

✔ Jean-Paul Droin

✔ Jean Dauvissat

✔ Verget

✔ Gérard Duplessis

✔ Christian Moreau Père et Fils

✔ Jean-Claude Bessin

✔ William Fèvre

✔ Domaine Laroche

✔ Long-Depaquit

✔ Billaud-Simon

Burgundy royalty: Côte d'Or

Most wine lovers associate the word "Burgundy" specifically with the wines from the Côte d'Or, the heart of the Burgundy region. The reds and whites of the Côte d'Or are the best that Burgundy has to offer — and they're priced accordingly.

So that you can spend your Burgundy dollars wisely, we recommend you stick to the following criteria, listed in order of importance, when choosing your red or white Burgundy wines:

✔ **The producer's reputation:** Consult recent newsletters, review the list later in this section, or ask a knowledgeable wine merchant.

✔ **The vintage:** The Burgundy region experiences considerable variation in quality and style from year to year.

✔ **The appellation:** The name of the commune and/or the vineyard, although significant, is invariably less important than the producer or the vintage.

Our top ten Côte d'Or Red Burgundy producers (in our rough order of preference) are as follows:

✔ Domaine (and Maison) Leroy

✔ Domaine de la Romanée-Conti

✔ Domaine du Comte de Vogüé

✔ Domaine Anne Gros

✔ Domaine Hubert Lignier

✔ Domaine Claude Dugat

- ✔ Domaine Robert Groffier
- ✔ Clos de Tart
- ✔ Domaine Joseph Roty
- ✔ Domaine Jean Grivot

A few of the outstanding Côte d'Or White Burgundy producers (listed in alphabetical order) are

- ✔ Domaine Louis Carillon & Fils
- ✔ Domaine Jean-François Coche-Dury
- ✔ Domaine des Comtes Lafon
- ✔ Domaine Leflaive
- ✔ Domaine Ramonet
- ✔ Domaine Étienne Sauzet

The Côte Chalonnaise: Affordable Burgundies

The Côte Chalonnaise district boasts five wine villages that are good sources of very decent, affordable red and white Burgundies. They're good values, and they're excellent choices in restaurants or for everyday drinking.

We recommend the following producers of Côte Chalonnaise wines (listed in alphabetical order):

- ✔ **Domaine Bertrand** (Montagny)
- ✔ **René Bourgeon** (Givry Blanc)
- ✔ **Domaine Jean-Claude Brelière** (Rully)
- ✔ **Domaine Michel Briday** (Rully)
- ✔ **Château de Chamirey** (Antonin Rodet — Mercurey Rouge and Blanc)
- ✔ **Château de Rully** (Antonin Rodet — both Rully Blanc and Rouge)

- **J. Faiveley** (Mercurey Rouge and Blanc; Rully Blanc; Montagny)
- **Château Genot-Boulanger** (Mercurey)
- **Domaine Joblot** (Givry)
- **Domaine Michel Juillot** (Mercurey Rouge and Blanc)
- **Olivier Leflaive Frères** (Rully Blanc; Mercurey Blanc)
- **Domaine Thierry Lespinasse** (Givry)
- **Domaine de la Rénarde** (Rully)

Everyday whites: The Mâcon

The city of Mâcon (*mah cawn*) is located at the southern end of the Mâconnais — a wine district that's directly south of the Côte Chalonnaise and north of Beaujolais. Almost all the Mâcon wine that's exported is white.

The wines of Mâcon and Mâcon-Villages (*mac cawn vee lahj*) are medium-bodied, fresh, crisp, lively, and almost always made without the use of oak. Drink them when they're young — within three years of the vintage.

The most famous Mâcon wine is undoubtedly Pouilly-Fuissé (*poo yee fwee say*), the most full-bodied and the most expensive wine of the Mâconnais. Pouilly-Fuissé wines come from a vineyard area around the villages of Pouilly and Fuissé and, unlike simpler Mâcon white wines, are usually aged in small oak barrels.

St.-Véran (*san veh rahn*) wines have about half the production (250,000 cases annually) of Pouilly-Fuissé and are far better values. These wines are similar to Pouilly-Fuissé but are less full-bodied.

Here are our recommended producers of Mâcon, Mâcon-Villages, Viré-Clessé, and St.-Véran wines, listed in our rough order of preference:

- ✔ Verget
- ✔ Domaine Jean Thévenet
- ✔ Domaine Valette
- ✔ Jean-Claude Thévenet
- ✔ Roger Lasserat
- ✔ Louis Latour
- ✔ Louis Jadot
- ✔ Joseph Drouhin
- ✔ Manciat-Poncet
- ✔ André Bonhomme
- ✔ Emilian Gillet
- ✔ Olivier Merlin

And here are our recommended producers of Pouilly-Fuissé wines, again listed in our rough order of preference:

- ✔ M. Vincent/Château Fuisse
- ✔ Daniel Barraud
- ✔ Domaine J.A. Ferrat
- ✔ Domaine Robert Denogent
- ✔ Verget
- ✔ Domaine Valette
- ✔ Manciat-Poncet
- ✔ Thierry Guérin
- ✔ Château de Beauregard

- Roger Lasserat
- Louis Latour
- Louis Jadot

Serving Burgundy

Red Burgundy from the Côte d'Or can be consumed when it's relatively young, after five or six years. Serve your red Burgundies slightly cool — about 60°F to 62°F (17°C) in a fine, wide-bowled glass. *Don't* decant red Burgundies; pour them straight from the bottle. Too much aeration causes you to lose some of your wine's wonderful aromas — one of its greatest qualities.

White Côte d'Or Burgundies are among the most long-lived white wines in the world. In good vintages, the best white Burgundies, such as Corton-Charlemagne or a *grand cru* Montrachet, can age for 20 years or more. Unlike red Burgundies, the better whites need time, often ten years or more, to really develop and open up. *Note:* We recommend decanting your serious white Burgundies; they truly benefit from the extra aeration.

Serve fine white Burgundies slightly cooler than red — about 55°F to 58°F (13°C to 15°C). You can't appreciate their wonderful, complex flavors when they're too cold. We enjoy our good white Burgundies in a wide-bowled glass, just slightly smaller than the glass we use for red Burgundies.

Beaujolais, the Fun Red

Administratively, Beaujolais is a district of the Burgundy region, but the red wine of Beaujolais is so different from those in the rest of Burgundy — made from a different grape variety grown in different soil and a warmer climate — that we consider Beaujolais to be a wine region in its own right, distinct from Burgundy.

Except for a small amount of Chardonnay, 99 percent of the Beaujolais vineyards are covered by a single grape variety, Gamay; all red Beaujolais wine derives entirely from Gamay. The Gamay variety makes wines that are fairly deep in color, with a bluish tinge. They tend to have light to medium body, relatively low acidity, moderate tannin, and aromas and flavors of red berries.

From frivolous to firm

Not all Beaujolais wine is the same. Soil differences throughout the region and subtle variations in wine-making technique cause the wines to vary considerably in style — from light-bodied, precocious wines at one end of the spectrum to denser, fuller-bodied wines at the other end. All these wines are dry.

Beaujolais and Beaujolais-Villages

The lightest wines, from the southern part of the region, usually carry the region's most basic appellation, "Beaujolais." These wines are generally light-bodied with low tannin and pronounced, youthful, fruity aromas and flavors; they're wines to drink young, in the first year after the harvest. Wines with the appellation Beaujolais Supérieur are basic Beaujolais wines that have a higher minimum alcohol content.

A separate type of Beaujolais comes from grapes grown in the territory of 39 villages in the northern part of the region: "Beaujolais-Villages" (*bo jho lay vee lahj*). These wines are fuller and more substantial than simple Beaujolais wines thanks to the schist and granite soils of the north — but they're still fruity, fresh, youthful wines for consuming young, until they're about two years old. Beaujolais-Villages wines account for 25 percent of all Beaujolais production.

Beaujolais Nouveau

Beaujolais Nouveau, *new Beaujolais,* is the lightest, fruitiest, most exuberant style of Beaujolais. It differs from other Beaujolais wines not according to where it comes from, but according to how it's made: with minimum aging and maximum personality. Beaujolais Nouveau is designed to be delicious when it's barely two months old.

Beaujolais Nouveau is the first French wine to be released from each year's new crop of grapes. By mid-November, the wine is already bottled and on its way to market. On the third Thursday of November the wine becomes legal: Wine drinkers all over the world open bottles to celebrate the harvest.

Cru Beaujolais

The best Beaujolais wines come from ten specific zones in the north. They carry the name of the area where the grapes grow; their official appellations don't use the word "Beaujolais" at all. (Many labels for the U.S. market do carry the words "Red Beaujolais Wine" in small print, however.)

The wines from these ten areas are known as *cru Beaujolais. Cru* Beaujolais wines are firmer, richer and more refined than other Beaujolais wines. But generalizations about these wines are problematic, because the *cru* wines vary in style from one *cru* to another.

The ten *cru* Beaujolais, from south to north, are

 ✔ **Brouilly** (*broo yee*)
 ✔ **Côte de Brouilly**

✔ **Régnié** (*ray nyay*)

✔ **Morgon** (*mor gohn*)

✔ **Chiroubles** (*sheh roob leh*)

✔ **Fleurie** (*flehr ee*)

✔ **Moulin-à-Vent** (*moo lahn ah vahn*)

✔ **Chénas** (*shay nahs*)

✔ **Juliénas** (*jool yay nahs*)

✔ **St.-Amour** (*sant ah more*)

Enjoying Beaujolais

Beaujolais is best when it's young, because with age it loses its distinctiveness. The lighter the style, the younger the wine should be. Here are some general guidelines:

✔ **Beaujolais Nouveau:** Drink as young as possible; it will still be drinkable at one or even two years old, but you sacrifice personality along the way.

✔ **Simple Beaujolais wines:** Ready from their release, about one month after the nouveau style, to about one year later.

✔ **Beaujolais-Villages:** Drinkable from about March of the year after the harvest until they're about two years old.

✔ **Lighter *cru* wines:** Drink within three years of the vintage.

✔ **Medium-bodied *cru* Beaujolais:** Best from one to four years after the vintage.

✔ **The fullest *crus*:** Drink four to seven years after the vintage, up to ten years for Moulin-à-Vent.

Sparkling Champagne

Is there a better-known, more popular wine in the world than Champagne? When it comes to sparkling wines, the sparkling wine people call "Champagne" has no peer.

Champagne is a white or rosé sparkling wine that starts its life like any other wine — as the fermented juice of grapes. But a subsequent, vital step transforms Champagne (and all the other serious sparkling wines of the world). Bottle the wine with yeast and a little sugar-wine solution, and it undergoes a second fermentation; this time, the bottle traps the carbon dioxide (a byproduct of fermentation) so that it takes the form of tiny bubbles in the wine. Voila! You have Champagne — at least you do if this process takes place in the Champagne region of France. And that's the catch. True Champagne comes only from this one wine region. All other bubbly wines are simply "sparkling wines" — no matter what they choose to call themselves on the label.

Champagne is made mainly from three grape varieties:

- ✔ Pinot Noir (a red wine variety)
- ✔ Pinot Meunier (a red variety related to Pinot Noir)
- ✔ Chardonnay (a white variety)

Most Champagnes — about 85 to 90 percent of them — are a blend of about two-thirds red grapes and one-third Chardonnay. A few Champagnes (less than 5 percent) are 100 percent Chardonnay (they're called *blanc de blancs*); fewer yet are 100 percent red grapes (and called *blanc de noirs*). Rosé Champagnes, a small category, are usually, but not always, made from a blend of white and red grapes.

Enormous variation exists among Champagnes. Some of them are sweeter than others, for example, or lighter, or more complex. We refer to the different types and tastes of Champagnes as the various *styles* of Champagnes. We tell you all about each style in the following sections.

Non-vintage, vintage, and prestige cuvées

After you understand these three styles, you can distinguish them from one another fairly easily. The challenge is that the labels don't tell you which type a Champagne is. Here's a thumbnail description of each:

- ✔ **Non-vintage Champagne:** The most common type by far, these wines are blends of wines from several years, and no vintage date appears on the label. They're called "non-vintage" because they don't derive from just *one* vintage. Non-vintage Champagnes are also known as "Classic" Champagnes — the least-expensive type (with a few exceptions).

- ✔ **Vintage Champagnes:** These are made from grapes of a single year, which is usually, but not always, a better-than-average year. The vintage year appears on the label.

- ✔ **Prestige *cuvées*:** These are the producers' best Champagnes, mainly vintage Champagnes but possibly non-vintage, and the most expensive type of Champagne. Cuvée Dom Pérignon and Roederer Cristal are examples.

Blanc de blancs, blanc de noirs, and rosé Champagnes

Although more than 90 percent of all Champagnes are a blend of at least two grape varieties and are white in color, three other types of Champagne exist:

- ✔ *Blanc de blancs* **Champagne:** *Blanc de blancs* Champagnes, made from Chardonnay only, are lighter-bodied, more acidic, and more elegant than other Champagnes. Many have vibrant, tart, lemony flavors. They tend to be slightly more expensive than other Champagnes, but they also age extremely well. Some of the most famous *blanc de blancs* Champagnes are Billecart-Salmon (*bee ay car sal mohn*) Blanc de Blancs, Deutz Blanc de Blancs, and Mumm de Cramant (*crah mahn*).

- ✔ *Blanc de noirs* **Champagne:** *Blanc de noirs* are the rarest type of Champagnes, especially among the larger Champagne houses. Typically golden in color, they're usually 100 percent Pinot Noir. This is the fullest-bodied type of Champagne and can accompany main courses at dinner very nicely.

- ✔ **Rosé Champagne:** Rosé Champagnes come in all different hues of pink and are always *brut* Champagnes, meaning they're always dry. They get their color from a little Pinot Noir wine that's added for that purpose. A couple popular rosé Champagnes are Billecart-Salmon (*sal mohn*) Brut Rosé and Gosset (*go say*) Grand Rosé Brut.

From dry to sweet: Brut, Extra Dry, and Demi-Sec Champagne

Most Champagnes benefit from a dosage (*doh sahj*), a wine-sugar solution added as a final adjustment to the wine after its second fermentation and aging; the dosage balances the wine's high acidity and makes the wine more palatable. Depending on the amount of sugar added, and the amount of counter-balancing acidity in the wine, you might or might not perceive the sweetness.

Technically, six different levels of dryness are permitted in Champagne, but, practically speaking, we see only three types: Brut, Extra Dry, and Demi-Sec.

Brut Champagnes

Brut Champagnes constitute the largest category of Champagnes, but they aren't a uniform category: The only way to determine how dry or sweet a Brut Champagne actually is, within the range allowed by law, is to know the producer's style. The driest Brut Champagnes are

- Bollinger
- Gosset (*go say*)
- Jacquesson
- Krug
- Bruno Paillard
- Salon (*sah loan*)

Extra Dry and Demi-Sec Champagnes

Extra Dry Champagnes are "on the dry side," but somewhat sweeter than Brut Champagnes. This category is really marketed only in the United States (perhaps due to our national sweet tooth?). In fact, one brand, Moët & Chandon's White Star (an Extra Dry Champagne) is the best-selling Champagne in the U.S.

The only Champagne that has enough sweetness for after dinner and/or dessert is Demi-Sec Champagne. Demi-Sec Champagnes aren't very common, but at least four houses (Moët & Chandon, Veuve Clicquot, Laurent-Perrier, and Louis Roederer) still make this style.

"House styles"

 We classify 25 major producers into three categories (listed alphabetically within the category) according to their house styles: light and elegant, medium-bodied, or full-bodied. The house styles of the producers are most evident in their non-vintage Brut (and Extra Dry) Champagnes, which they produce every year, and which make up the largest part of their production. Although producers do try to express their house styles in their vintage Champagnes, the influence of the climate in a particular vintage year can sometimes mask the house style.

✔ **Light, elegant style:**

- Billecart-Salmon
- Henriot
- Jacquesson
- Bruno Paillard
- Perrier-Jouët
- Piper-Heidsieck
- Pommery
- Ruinart
- Taittinger

✔ **Medium-bodied style:**

- Cattier
- Deutz
- Charles Heidsieck

- Moët & Chandon
- Philipponnat
- Pol Roger

✔ **Full-bodied style:**

- Bollinger
- Gosset
- Alfred Gratien
- Krug
- Louis Roederer
- Salon
- Veuve Clicquot Ponsardin

Serving Champagne

 Good Champagne glasses are crucial for maximum enjoyment of your bubbly. The glass should be tall and slender, with a long stem (so that you don't hold the glass by the bowl and warm up your Champagne). A flute-shaped glass is fine for non-vintage Champagne. For vintage Champagne and prestige cuvées, we recommend a tulip-shaped glass (wider than a flute), which benefits the wine's aromas. Actually, tulip-shaped glasses (about 9 to 10 inches tall, including the stem) can be used for all Champagnes.

Serve Champagne cold (about 45°F to 48°F; 7°C to 9°C). Vintage Champagnes and prestige cuvées, which have more complex flavors, can be a bit warmer (50°F to 53°F; 10°C to 12°C). You can chill your Champagne to the desired temperature with at least four hours in the fridge, or 30 minutes in a tall ice bucket (with half ice and half cold water).

When serving, pour the Champagne slowly into the glass so the fizziness has time to settle down; this way, you won't shortchange your guests with a tiny pour. Fill the glass about two-thirds of the way and refill it when just a little bit of Champagne remains in the glass (refilling restores the wine's effervescence). Refill frequently.

After you pour your first round of Champagne, put the bottle into an ice bucket or back into the refrigerator; warm Champagne doesn't taste too good! Also, the bubbles dissipate more quickly at warmer temperatures. If you have any Champagne left over, close the bottle with a Champagne stopper and put it back into the fridge. It should keep well for two or three days.

Chapter 4

Valuing the Variety of Italian Wine

In This Chapter

▶ Recognizing why Italy is winemaking heaven

▶ Diving into the wines of the Piedmont region

▶ Sampling Chianti in Tuscany and a variety of wines in Southern Italy

*W*hen most people think of Italy, they think of food. (History, art, or fast cars might be other associations — but food would have to be right up there, near the top of the list.)

As central as food is to Italy's personality, so is wine. For most Italians, wine *is* food, no less essential to every meal than bread or family. Wine, in fact, *is* family, and community, because nearly every Italian either knows someone who makes wine or makes wine himself.

Italy, Born to Make Wine

The Italian peninsula, with its fan-like top and its long,
boot-like body, has the most recognizable shape of
any country on earth. But its recognition exceeds its
actual size. Italy is a small land; the whole country is
less than three-quarters the size of California.

Despite its small size, Italy's role in the world of wine
is huge:

- ✔ Italy produces more wine than any other country on earth, in many years. (When Italy isn't
  the world's number one wine producer, it's
  number two, behind France.) Italy's annual
  wine production is generally about 1.5 billion
  gallons — that's the equivalent of more than
  8 billion bottles! Nearly 30 percent of all the
  world's wine comes from Italy.

- ✔ Italy has more vineyard land than any other
  country except Spain. Vines grow in every nook
  and cranny of the peninsula and the islands.

- ✔ Italy boasts dozens of native grape varieties,
  many of which are successful only in Italy.

- ✔ Italy produces hundreds of wines — nearly
  1,000 different types, we'd say.

Italy consists of 20 different wine regions, which you
can see in Figure 4-1.

Diverse conditions, diverse wines

What makes Italy an ideal and unique territory for
growing grapes is precisely its improbable combination of natural conditions:

- ✔ The range of latitudes creates a wide variety of
  climatic conditions from north to south.

✔ The foothills of the mountains provide slopes ideal for vineyards, as well as higher altitudes for cool climate grape growing.

✔ The varied terrain — seacoast, hills, and mountains — within many regions provides a diversity of growing conditions even within single regions.

✔ The segregated nature of the regions has enabled local grape varieties to survive in near isolation.

Figure 4-1: Italy's wine regions.

When it comes to wine production, Italy's odd situation is a formula for variety (and a formula for confusion on the part of those trying to master Italian wines!). Different grape varieties make different wines in different regions. And the same grape variety makes different wines in different parts of a single region. In a nutshell, that's why Italy makes so many different wines.

Italian wine styles today

The fundamental style of Italian wine derives from the fact that Italians view wine as a mealtime beverage; a wine's first responsibility is to go well with food. The prototypical Italian red or white wine has the following characteristics:

- ✔ High acidity, which translates as crispness in the whites and firmness in the reds (high-acid wines are very food-friendly)
- ✔ No sweetness
- ✔ Fairly subdued, subtle aromas and flavors (so as not to compete with food)
- ✔ Light to medium body (although many full-bodied Italian wines do exist)

If you imagine such a wine, you can understand that it's a wine without illusions of grandeur, a straightforward beverage that might not win a wine competition but is a welcome dinner companion.

Variations on the prototype in recent years have included some of the following characteristics:

- ✔ More concentrated flavor and slightly fuller body, due to greater ripeness in the grapes (thanks to improved vineyard practices)
- ✔ Smoky or toasty aromas and flavors from small oak barrels

> ✔ Fruitier aromas and flavors — although the wines are still much less fruity than, say, the typical Californian or Australian wine

About two-thirds of all Italian wine is red. Every region makes red wine, even the cool northern regions and especially the South. But Italy makes plenty of white wine, too — particularly Northeast and Central Italy. Rosé wine is only a minor category.

Italy's production of sparkling wine is considerable, especially in the North. Italian sparkling wines include sweet styles, such as Asti, and fully dry styles. Dessert wines are a serious specialty of some regions. These sweet wines include wines from grapes dried after the harvest (to concentrate their sugar); wines from late-harvested grapes affected with *noble rot* (a fungus known also as *botrytis cinerea* that dehydrates the berries and concentrates their sugars and flavors); and wines that are fortified with alcohol to preserve their natural sweetness.

A note on names

If you can show that your climate, soil, or other natural condition (including human factors, such as tradition) is different from that of a nearby area, then you presumably make a different type of wine than that other area — and, upon request, the authorities can give you a unique, official name for your type of wine.

Italy's official wine names are called DOC or DOCG names:

> ✔ DOC stands for *Denominazione di Origine Controllata* (dae-no-mee-naht-zee-*oh*-nae-dee-oh-*ree*-gee-nae-con-trol-*lah*-tah), which translates as "controlled (or protected) place name"; the long Italian phrase appears on the wine label.

✔ DOCG stands for *Denominazione di Origine
Controllata e Garantita* (. . . ae-gah-rahn-*tee*-tah),
which translates as "controlled and guaranteed
place name"; this even longer Italian phrase
appears on the labels of DOCG wines.

Every DOC or DOCG wine comes from a specific
place that's defined by law, is made from specific grapes stipulated by the law (although
sometimes the law gives producers a lot of
leeway in their choice of grapes), is aged for a
certain length of time, and so forth. In the end,
a wine that carries a DOC or DOCG name should
taste more or less the way the law says that
wine should taste, although the official taste
descriptions are loose; for example, they might
say that a particular wine should taste "dry,
crisp, harmonious, and slightly tannic." Lots of
room for interpretation there.

The Wines of Piedmont

Piedmont, Italy's northwestern-most region, is remote
from the rest of mainland Italy. The remoteness of
this part of Italy has helped to preserve local traditions, local cuisine, and local wine styles. And we're
not just talking about quaint local color: Some of the
wines from northwestern Italy are among Italy's very
greatest, period.

Piedmont — specifically the Barolo and Barbaresco
districts — was the first region in Italy to recognize
the importance of making separate wines from excep-
tional vineyards, a concept that Burgundy and other
regions of France had practiced for some time.
Producers such as Vietti and Prunotto began making
single-vineyard Barolos and Barbarescos in 1961.

About 90 percent of Piedmont's wine comes from the southern part of the region. This production falls roughly into the following two areas:

- The Alba area, in southcentral Piedmont, which includes the Langhe Hills area and the Roero area

- The Asti/Alessandria area, in southeast Piedmont, extending south of the Po River to the border with Liguria, and including the Monferrato Hills

Piedmont boasts three major red grape varieties and two major white varieties:

- **Nebbiolo:** A noble but difficult, late-ripening red variety that nowhere in the world grows as well and makes such superb wine (when conditions are right) as it does in the Langhe (*lahn*-gae) hills around the town of Alba.

- **Barbera:** A native red Piedmontese variety that until a few decades ago was Italy's most planted red variety. In Piedmont, it grows mainly in the Asti and Alba areas, making serious as well as everyday wines.

- **Dolcetto:** A spicy red variety seldom seen outside Piedmont. It's widely grown in the Alba and southeastern areas of the region.

- **Moscato:** A world-renowned white grape with floral aromas and flavors. It's a specialty of the Asti area.

- **Cortese:** A grape that makes delicately flavored dry white wines. It's a specialty of the Gavi area.

Wines of the Alba area

The Alba wine zone consists of two areas in south-central Piedmont, the Langhe hills and the Roero, which surround the town of Alba. This fairly small area produces Northern Italy's two greatest red wines — Barolo and Barbaresco — as well as several others of note.

Barolo

Derived entirely from the Nebbiolo grape, a well-made Barolo from a good vintage is one of the greatest red wines in the world. It's powerful and full-bodied, with all sorts of intriguing aromas and flavors — ripe strawberries, tar, mint and/or eucalyptus, licorice, camphor, tobacco, chocolate, roses, spices, vanilla, and white truffles — and it only gets better with age.

Five communities produce most (87 percent) of Barolo, and most of the best Barolo:

- La Morra
- Barolo
- Serralunga d'Alba
- Castiglione Falletto
- Monforte d'Alba

Not counting the producers' individual imprints, two different types of Barolo exist, according to the location of the vineyards:

- The Barolo wines of the Serralunga (eastern) Valley — which includes the communities of Serralunga d'Alba, Castiglione Falletto, and Monforte d'Alba — tend to be more austere, powerful, and long-lived. They're more tannic and more full-bodied than other Barolos. Also, they generally have more extract (solid grape matter) and alcohol, and require long aging — 12 to 15 years — to develop and mature.

✔ The Barolo wines of the Central (western)
  Valley — basically the largest community,
  La Morra, which accounts for about one-third
  of all Barolo wine, and part of the community of
  Barolo — often have more perfumed aromas,
  such as white truffles. They're typically more
  elegant (complete with a velvety texture), less
  full-bodied, and less tannic than the Barolos of
  the Serralunga Valley. They're also usually
  ready to drink sooner — often within eight to
  ten years of their vintage date.

Following are our very favorite Barolo producers
(listed alphabetically) and the communes where
most, or all, of their vineyards are located.

✔ **Giacomo Conterno** (Serralunga d'Alba)

✔ **Gaja** (Serralunga d'Alba; La Morra)

✔ **Bruno Giacosa** (Serralunga d'Alba; Castiglione
  Falletto)

✔ **Bartolo Mascarello** (Barolo)

✔ **Giuseppe Mascarello** (Castiglione Falletto;
  Monforte d'Alba)

✔ **Giuseppe Rinaldi** (Barolo; La Morra)

✔ **Luciano Sandrone** (Barolo)

✔ **Paolo Scavino** (Castiglione Falletto)

✔ **Vietti** (Castiglione Falletto)

Barbaresco

The other great red wine of the Langhe hills,
Barbaresco (bahr-bah-*res*-co), also a DOCG wine, is
very similar to Barolo. Both Barolo and Barbaresco
are made entirely from Nebbiolo, share similar soils
and climate (because they're within ten miles of each
other), and many producers make both wines using
similar production methods.

Barbaresco is a sturdy, austere, powerful wine, generally only slightly less full-bodied than Barolo: Its minimum alcohol content is slightly less (12.5 percent, compared to 13 percent for Barolo), and its minimum aging at the winery (two years minimum, four for *riservas*) is one year less than Barolo's.

The aromas and flavors of Barbaresco wines are very much the same as those of Barolo. But Barbaresco is more elegant, typically less austere, and more accessible in its youth. For this reason, it's generally a better choice in restaurants, especially when most of the available wines are from recent vintages.

Because Barbaresco has fewer producers than Barolo, in a smaller, more consistent territory, it's a more consistently reliable wine, generally speaking.

Of course, some differences do exist among Barbarescos according to their vineyard area (remember that winemaking style can camouflage the characteristics of the vineyard area, however):

- The community of Neive, on the next hill east of Barbaresco, produces the most full-bodied, tannic Barbarescos in the region. Neive accounts for almost 31 percent of Barbaresco and is the home of the great Bruno Giacosa, as well as Fratelli Cigliuti and the historic Castello di Neive.

- The wines of the Barbaresco community tend to be a bit lighter in color and lighter-bodied than those of Neive, but they're known for their perfumed aromas and their structure.

- Treiso d'Alba (or simply Treiso), south of Barbaresco, is the least-known of the three areas. Its Barbarescos tend to be lighter-bodied than the others, and they're known for their finesse and their elegance.

Here are our favorite Barbaresco producers, listed alphabetically along with the name of the communes where most, or all, of their vineyards are located.

- ✔ **Ceretto, also known as Bricco Asili** (Barbaresco)
- ✔ **Fratelli Cigliuti** (Neive)
- ✔ **Angelo Gaja** (Barbaresco)
- ✔ **Bruno Giacosa** (Neive)
- ✔ **Marchesi di Gresy** (Barbaresco)
- ✔ **Roagna, also known as I Paglieri** (Barbaresco)
- ✔ **Albino Rocca** (Barbaresco)
- ✔ **Bruno Rocca** (Barbaresco)
- ✔ **La Spinetta** (Neive)
- ✔ **La Spinona** (Barbaresco)

Barbera d'Alba

Barbera d'Alba (bar-*bae*-rah-*dahl*-bah) is generally the finest and most serious of the three red varietal wines that get their name from the town of Alba. Barbera is a strange variety. It has lots of pigmentation and very high acidity but almost no tannin in its skins and seeds. Its wines are therefore dark in color but crisp and refreshing, rather like white wines, instead of being firm and mouth-drying like most reds — but its berry-cherry and spicy flavors are red wine all the way.

 Barbera d'Alba is enjoyable both young and with age, up to about 15 years, to our taste — although as it ages beyond about 8 years, it loses its spicy vibrancy and becomes a more normalized red wine. Simple, inexpensive Barbera is our favorite wine with pizza, but the best examples are really too good for such casual food. Barbera is terrific with pasta with tomato sauce, spicy foods, bitter greens, and hearty dishes.

Our favorite producers of Barbera d'Alba, listed alphabetically, are as follows:

- Elio Altare
- Elvio Cogno
- Aldo Conterno
- Giacomo Conterno
- Gaja
- Manzone
- Marcarini
- Bartolo Mascarello
- Giuseppe Mascarello
- Moccagatta
- Prunotto
- Giuseppi Rinaldi
- Paolo Scavino
- Vietti

Dolcetto d'Alba

Dolcetto d'Alba (dohl-*chet*-toh-*dahl*-bah) comes from vineyards in the Langhe hills and is made entirely from Dolcetto, which ripens earlier than other red varieties of the area. Dolcetto d'Alba is also earlier maturing as a wine than Barbera d'Alba or Nebbiolo d'Alba (described in the next section). In meals, it's usually served before Barbera — to accompany the five or six (or eight) antipasto courses of a typical Piedmontese meal.

Dolcetto has lower acidity than Barbera, but it's still acidic, as any self-respecting Italian wine should be; its acid suits it well to food. It's more tannic than Barbera — a dry, medium-bodied, rich-textured wine with aromas and flavors of black pepper and ripe berry fruit.

 We love to drink Dolcetto d'Alba with some of the same kinds of foods as Barbera — pizza, somewhat spicy dishes, earthy vegetarian foods — but it's also terrific with casual meals such as chef salads, cold cuts, sandwiches, or turkey burgers. Dolcetto d'Alba is best when it's no more than three years old, in our opinion.

Many Barolo producers also make Dolcetto d'Alba; our favorite producers, in alphabetical order, are

- Elio Altare
- Clerico
- Elvio Cogno (a specialty)
- Giacomo Conterno
- Conterno-Fantino
- Marcarini
- Ratti
- Sandrone
- Vietti

Nebbiolo d'Alba

To our way of thinking, Nebbiolo d'Alba (nehb-bee-*oh*-loh-*dahl*-bah) runs a distant third among the three Alba varietal wines. Not that it's not a perfectly fine, well-made wine most of the time; we just prefer to experience Nebbiolo in its most dramatic, highest-quality expression — as Barolo and Barbaresco. Nebbiolo d'Alba lacks the intensity and flair of those wines, and instead is just a good, medium-bodied, firm red wine with delicate flavors of tar, red fruits, and herbs.

Nebbiolo d'Alba is a relatively light style of Nebbiolo for drinking young; the wine must age only one year before release. Its best drinkability period is three to seven years from the vintage, in our opinion. Also to its advantage, it's relatively inexpensive.

One Barolo producer who makes a specialty of producing fine Nebbiolo d'Alba is **Tenuta Carretta**.

The wines of Asti and Alessandria

East and north of the Alba area are the provinces of Asti and Alessandria. Nebbiolo recedes in importance in Asti and Alessandria, and Barbera comes strongly to the foreground — along with a minor red variety called Grignolino (gree-n'yoh-*lee*-no), the red Malvasia, the white Cortese (cor-*tae*-sae) grape, and, above all, Moscato.

Asti is a famous name around the world, even to those who've never visited that city. The reason is the DOCG wine called Asti, Italy's flagship sparkling wine and one of the most unique sparkling wines in the world. Asti is made entirely from the Moscato grape — the Muscat à Petits Grains type, the best Muscat variety of all. It's a sweet, absolutely delicious bubbly with rich floral, peachy flavors and lots of acidity to balance its sweetness.

Asti is all about freshness. After the wine is about two or three years old, it starts to taste richer and somewhat heavy — still tasty, but no longer at its best. To complicate the matter, however, Asti doesn't carry a vintage date, so you don't know *how* old a particular bottle really is. Our suggestion is to purchase Asti from a store that sells a lot of it, and to purchase a brand that sells well, because the turnover assures freshness. Our favorite brands are

Fontanafredda, Martini & Rossi, and **Cinzano,** but freshness is even more important than which brand you choose. And make sure the wine is genuine Asti; imitations do exist!

A companion wine to Asti — made from the same grapes in the same vineyard areas and covered under the same DOCG — is Moscato d'Asti (mo-*scah*-toh-*dahs*-tee). This wine is quite similar to Asti except that it's just *frizzante* — lightly bubbly, or fizzy — rather than sparkling, and its flavors are more delicate than Asti's. It's also even lower in alcohol — generally from 5 to 7.5 percent. Freshness is even more crucial for Moscato d'Asti than it is for Asti, but fortunately the wines are vintage dated. Buy the youngest vintage possible, and never buy any vintage that's more than two years old.

Our favorite Moscato d'Asti is **Cascinetta,** made by Vietti; **La Spinetta** is a well-regarded brand, but the wine is slightly less delicate. Other good brands are Ceretto's **Santo Stefano, Piero Gatti, Dante Rivetti,** and **Paolo Saracco.**

The Wines of Tuscany

Tuscany sits on Italy's western coast and is quite hilly (refer to Figure 4-1). The altitude of the hills tempers the summer heat, which can otherwise be sweltering.

About 50 percent of Tuscany's wine production is DOC or DOCG. Tuscany has six DOCG wines and 29 DOCs (depending on how you count them); the vast majority (80 percent) of this classified-level production is red wine. The six DOCG wines are

- **Chianti** (key-*ahn*-tee)
- **Chianti Classico**

✔ **Brunello di Montalcino** (brew-*nel*-lo-dee-mahn-tahl-*chee*-no)

✔ **Carmignano Rosso** (car-mee-*nyah*-no)

✔ **Vino Nobile di Montepulciano** (*vee*-no-*no*-bee-lae-dee-mahn-tae-pool-chee-*ah*-no)

✔ **Vernaccia di San Gimignano** (ver-*nahch*-cha-dee-san-gee-mee-*nyah*-no)

Of these wines, only Vernaccia di San Gimignano is white.

Sangiovese is the main red grape variety of Tuscany, not just quantitatively but also qualitatively speaking. Many clones of Sangiovese exist; besides broad families of Sangiovese, such as the top-quality Sangiovese Grosso and the ordinary Sangiovese di Romagna, numerous local clones have evolved in each of the districts where the grape has traditionally grown, in response to local conditions. Sangiovese's many mutations explain why it has several different names or nicknames in Tuscany, such as Brunello, Prugnolo Gentile, and Morellino.

The next most important red variety in quality terms is Cabernet Sauvignon; this variety has grown in the region for at least 250 years but has become especially popular since the late 1970s.

Trebbiano is the leading white variety of the region in terms of acreage planted — and the main reason that Tuscan white wines are far less exciting than the reds. The highest-quality Tuscan white wines derive from the Vernaccia grape, grown around San Gimignano.

The land of Chianti

Chianti is not just Tuscany's most famous wine — it's Italy's most famous wine, and one of the most famous wines in the entire world. But Chianti is not just one type of wine. The name embodies wines from several subzones, which vary quite a lot in richness and quality; it also covers wines for drinking young and age-worthy wines; inexpensive wines and pricey wines. What these wines have in common is that they're all red, and they're all based on the Sangiovese grape.

Chianti Classico

Chianti Classico is not only the heartland of Tuscany — the original Chianti area, situated at the very center of Tuscany — it's also the emotional heart of the region. The zone is populated by serious and skilled winemakers who care deeply about their land and their wines, and who infect wine lovers all over the world with their passion.

Chianti Classico encompasses four *communes,* or communities, in their entirety — Greve, Radda, Gaiole, and Castellina — as well as portions of five others. More than 700 grape growers farm the 24,700 acres of vineyards in this area.

As generalizations go, most Chianti Classico wines are medium-bodied rather than full-bodied, firm rather than soft, with a medium amount of dry tannin, and medium to high acidity. Tart cherry or ripe cherry are the main aroma/flavor descriptors, sometimes with delicate floral or nutty notes. One characteristic of Chianti that strikes us is that the wines are fairly inexpressive in the front of your mouth; all their action happens in the middle and rear. They're completely different from most New World reds, whose richness is evident as soon as you put them in your mouth.

The average quality level of Chianti Classico wines is quite high, and we therefore admire the wines of many dozens of producers. Here are a few of our favorites, as well as the name of the commune where they're located:

✔ **Barone Ricasoli, formerly Castello di Brolio** (Gaiole)

✔ **Castellare di Castellina** (Castellina)

✔ **Castello dei Rampolla** (Panzano)

✔ **Castello di Ama** (Gaiole)

✔ **Castello di Fonterutoli** (Castellina)

✔ **Castello di Volpaia** (Radda)

✔ **Fattoria di Felsina** (Castelnuovo Berardegna)

✔ **Fontodi** (Panzano)

✔ **Isole e Olena** (Barberino Val d'Elsa)

✔ **Marchesi Antinori** (San Casciano Val di Pesa)

✔ **La Massa** (Panzano)

✔ **Monsanto** (Barberino Val d'Elsa)

✔ **Podere Il Palazzino** (Gaiole)

✔ **Ruffino** (various estates)

✔ **San Giusto a Rentennano** (Gaiole)

Chianti

The Chianti DOCG designation applies to all Chianti wines other than those made from grapes grown in the Chianti Classico area. This appellation covers wines from six specific subzones, as well as wines from peripheral areas. Wines from individual subzones may carry the name of that subzone on their labels, whereas wines from the other areas, or wines combining grapes from more than one subzone, simply carry the appellation Chianti DOCG.

The best Chianti wines are those from the following subzones:

✔ **Chianti Colli Pisane** (*coh*-lee-pee-*sah*-nae): The westernmost area, in the province of Pisa

✔ **Chianti Colli Fiorentini** (fee-or-en-*tee*-nee): Literally, "Florentine hills," north of Chianti Classico, in the province of Florence

✔ **Chianti Colli Senesi** (seh-*nae*-see): The Siena hills, the southernmost part

✔ **Chianti Colli Aretini** (ah-rae-*tee*-nee): The Arezzo hills, in the eastern part of the zone

✔ **Chianti Montalbano** (mon-tahl-*bah*-no): The northwest part of the zone

✔ **Chianti Rufina** (*roo*-fee-nah): The northeastern part of the zone

Of these areas, the Rufina zone probably ranks highest for the quality of its wines — and is also the one area whose wines are generally available in the United States. Some Rufina wines, such as the best of Selvapiana and Frescobaldi, are among the finest of all Chiantis.

Because Chianti Classico truly dominates the export market for all types of Chianti, our list of recommended producers of Chianti DOCG is short. We list these producers alphabetically, with their subzone in parentheses:

✔ **Fattoria di Basciano** (Rufina)

✔ **Tenuta di Capezzana** (Montalbano)

✔ **Castello di Farnatella** (Colli Senesi)

✔ **Marchesi de' Frescobaldi** (Rufina)

✔ **Chigi Saracini** (Colli Senesi)

✔ **Fattoria Selvapiana** (Rufina)

✔ **Fattoria di Manzano** (Colli Aretini)

✔ **Fattoria di Petrolo** (Colli Aretini)

Vernaccia di San Gimignano

The vineyards of San Gimignano (sahn-gee-me-_n'yah_-no) lie within the Chianti Colli Senesi area, but the local pride is the DOCG white wine, Vernaccia (ver-_nahtch_-chah).

Vernaccia di San Gimignano is Tuscany's finest type of white wine — and has been for seven centuries. It derives at least 90 percent from the Vernaccia grape variety, which is famous only here. Generally, Vernaccia is a fairly full-bodied, dry, soft white, with honey, mineral, and earthy flavors, but it sometimes is quite fruity.

The wine varies quite a lot in style according to its winemaking. Some producers ferment or age the wine in small French oak barrels, which gives the wine a toastiness or a creaminess that it doesn't otherwise have. Other producers make the wine un-oaked, so that the mineral aromas and flavors shine through more clearly. Some producers make more than one Vernaccia wine, each a different style.

We recommend the following producers of Vernaccia di San Gimignano, listed alphabetically:

- Baroncini
- Vincenzo Cesani
- Fattoria di Cusona
- Casale-Falchini
- La Lastra
- Montenidoli
- Mormoraia
- Palagetto
- Giovanni Panizzi

✔ Fattoria Il Paradiso

✔ Fattoria San Quirico

✔ Teruzzi & Puthod

✔ Fratelli Vagnoni

Monumental Montalcino

In terms of international renown, the Montalcino (mon-tal-*chee*-no) area is Tuscany's second most important wine zone, after Chianti Classico. In terms of quality, however, it's Tuscany's star.

Montalcino's signature wine is Brunello (brew-*nel*-lo) di Montalcino, a hefty red wine made entirely from Sangiovese. (Brunello is the local, but unofficial, name for Sangiovese.) In the isolated hills of Montalcino, Sangiovese ripens better than elsewhere in Tuscany, giving wines with more color, body, extract, tannin, and richness than other wines based on the same variety.

Brunello di Montalcino is considered one of Italy's two best wines. It was the first wine to earn DOCG status, in 1980, and it's generally among Italy's most expensive wines. But production is small: Only about 333,000 cases of Brunello di Montalcino are made each year.

Since its earliest conception, Brunello di Montalcino has been a wine for aging. Some wines from good vintages not only can age for 50 years or more, but in fact need a couple of decades to lose the fire of youth and become harmonious. The DOCG regulations echo the wine's potential by requiring that Brunello age for four years before it can be released — the longest minimum aging period for any wine in Italy.

Traditional-minded producers age their wine for three years or more in large, old casks, producing more austere wines, whereas the most avant-garde producers age some of their Brunello in small barrels of French oak (and practice other non-traditional wine-making techniques) to fix a certain fruitiness in their wine. In either case, almost every Brunello is best with at least ten years of age from the vintage.

Here we name our favorite producers of Brunello di Montalcino, in alphabetical order:

- ✔ Altesino
- ✔ Castello Banfi
- ✔ Biondi-Santi (expensive)
- ✔ Canalicchio di Sopra
- ✔ Case Basse of Soldera (very expensive)
- ✔ Castelgiocondo
- ✔ Ciacci Piccolomini
- ✔ Costanti
- ✔ Il Greppone Mazzi
- ✔ Pertimali di Livio Sassetti
- ✔ Poggio Antico
- ✔ Il Poggione
- ✔ La Torre

The Wines of Southern Italy

Southern Italy has a proud wine history. The area has produced wine for more than 4,000 years; in 2000 B.C., when Phoenician traders arrived in what is today the region of Apulia, a local wine industry was already thriving! The Greeks later dubbed Southern Italy "The Land of Wine."

Campania: Revival begins

Campania sits along Italy's western coast, on the Tyrrhenian Sea (refer to Figure 4-1). One of the key assets of the region is the red grape variety Aglianico (ah-l'yee-*ah*-nee-co), which has proven to be one of the great, noble grapes of Italy. Also, two white varieties, Fiano and Greco di Tufo, make some of the very best, long-lived white wines in the country.

The best of Campania's DOC wines can be grouped geographically into three areas:

- ✔ The Irpinia hills of Avellino, in central Campania
- ✔ The coastal hills and islands around Naples
- ✔ The northern hills of the region

The wines of Avellino

Campania's three greatest wines come from the Irpinia hills around the city of Avellino, the capital of the Avellino province: the red Taurasi, and two DOC whites, Fiano di Avellino and Greco di Tufo.

- ✔ **Taurasi:** Taurasi (touw-*rah*-see) must be at least 85 percent Aglianico, with up to 15 percent other red varieties, but in practice, most of the better Taurasi wines are 100 percent Aglianico. Taurasi is a wine that demands aging, not unlike the other great Italian reds (Barolo, Barbaresco, and Brunello). In good vintages, this complex, powerful, and tannic wine is at its best after 15 to 20 years. Mastroberardino's finest Taurasi is the single-vineyard "Radici"; other good Taurasi wines are made by Feudi di San Gregorio and Terredora.

- ✔ **Fiano di Avellino:** Fiano di Avellino must have at least 85 percent Fiano grapes, with the balance Greco and/or Coda di Volpe and/or Trebbiano

Toscano. At its best, Fiano di Avellino is Southern Italy's top dry white wine — and one of the best in the entire country. It's a delicately flavored wine with aromas of pear and toasted hazelnuts, which become more pronounced with age. Unlike most dry white wines, Fiano di Avellino is best with at least five or six years of aging and will be fine for up to 15, in good vintages. Wines to look for include Terredora's single-vineyard Terre di Dora, Mastroberardino's single-vineyard Vignadora, and Feudi di San Gregorio's Pietracalda.

✔ **Greco di Tufo:** Greco di Tufo (*greh-co-dee-too-foh*) wines must derive at least 85 percent from Greco, with the balance Coda di Volpe. Greco di Tufo wines are more intensely fruity and crisper than Fiano di Avellino, which are more subtle and a bit softer. Greco di Tufo is usually ready to drink after three or four years, but it can age for at least 10 to 12 years. Look for the Greco di Tufo wines of Feudi di San Gregorio, Mastroberardino, and Terredora.

Wines of the coastal hills and islands around Naples

The coastal hills and islands around Naples have seven DOC wines.

✔ **Ischia** (*ees*-key-ah): White wines dominate production, with D'Ambra Vini d'Ischia making the island's best. Ischia Bianco is mainly Forastera, with Biancolella and other white grapes; the same varieties also make a Bianco *spumante,* and each of these two grapes makes a varietal wine. Ischia Rosso is a dry red mainly from Guarnaccia (in the Grenache family) and Piedirosso (known locally as Pér'e Palummo); Piedirosso also makes a varietal wine and a *passito.*

✔ **Capri** (*cah*-pree): Capri has two wines: Capri Bianco (mainly Falanghina and Greco, with up to 20 percent Biancolella) and Capri Rosso (mainly Piedirosso).

✔ **Vesuvio:** Also called Lacryma Christi del Vesuvio (*lah*-cree-mah-*chree*-sti-de-veh-*soo*-vee-oh), this wine comes from vineyards on the slopes of Mount Vesuvius, east of Naples, overlooking the Bay of Naples. The basic wines, with less than 12 percent alcohol, carry the simpler Vesuvio DOC; the white, red, or rosé wines from riper grapes are Lacryma Christi ("tears of Christ") del Vesuvio. The Bianco is mainly Verdeca and Coda di Volpe, with up to 20 percent Greco and/or Falanghina; the Rosso and Rosato are mainly Piedirosso and Sciascinoso, with up to 20 percent Aglianico. All three Lacryma Christi wines can also be *spumante*.

✔ **Campi Flegrei** (*cahm*-pee-*fleh*-grae): Of Campania's newer DOC zones, this area has the most promise. Campi Flegrei Bianco is a dry white made mainly from Falanghina, Biancolella, and Coda di Volpe varieties; Campi Flegrei Falanghina is a dry white varietal — or a *spumante* — derived at least 90 percent from that variety. Campi Flegrei Rosso is a dry red (or *novello* style) mainly from Piedirosso, Aglianico, and Sciascinoso grapes. Campi Flegrei Piedirosso — dry or *passito* — must contain at least 90 percent of this variety.

✔ **Costa d'Amalfi** (*cohs*-tah-dah-*mahl*-fee): The Costa d'Amalfi DOC features Bianco, Rosso, and Rosato wines. The Bianco is at least 60 percent Falanghina and Biancolella; the Rosso and Rosato are at least 60 percent Piedirosso and Sciascinoso.

✔ **Penisola Sorrentina** (peh-*nee*-so-lahf-sor-ren-*tee*-nah): The Sorrento Peninsula zone is known for its fizzy red wines, but it has lost many of its

vineyards due to Naples' expansion. Penisola
Sorrentina Bianco is mainly Falanghina,
Biancolella, and/or Greco; the Rosso and Rosso
frizzante naturale are mainly Piedirosso,
Sciascinoso, and/or Aglianico.

✔ **Asprinio di Aversa** (ahs-_pree_-nee-oh-dee-ah-
vehr- sa): This wine zone makes a dry white
wine from at least 85 percent Asprinio grapes;
in its more popular form, Asprinio di Aversa is
a dry _spumante,_ from 100 percent Asprinio.
Aversa has been a declining wine area that
hopes the blessing of DOC status can revive it.

Campania's northern hills

Northern Campania is dominated by the Apennine
Mountains and their foothills. The region now has
seven DOC wines:

✔ **Falerno del Massico** (fah-_ler_-no-del-_mah_-see-co):
Three styles of Falerno del Massico exist: a
Bianco, a Rosso, and a Primitivo. Villa Matilde
and Fontana Galardi are two leading wineries.

✔ **Gallucio** (gahl-_loo_-cho): Gallucio's wines are
similar to Falerno's, but they tend to be a bit
lighter and have more aromatic finesse.

✔ **Solopaca** (so-lo-_pah_-cah): Six types of wine carry
the Solopaca DOC: a Rosso, Rosato, Bianco, two
varietal wines, and a _spumante._

✔ **Taburno** (tah-_bur_-no): Taburno has a varietal
Aglianico (Rosso or Rosato), Falanghina, Greco,
and Coda di Volpe (all whites), and Piedirosso.

✔ **Sant'Agata dei Goti** (sahnt-_ahg_-ah-tah-dae-_go_-
tee): A Bianco, Rosso, _novello,_ and Rosato — all
from the same varieties (no, we didn't make a
mistake!). Those varieties are Aglianico and
Piedirosso, both reds (other non-aromatic red

varieties may be added); the Bianco is made using only the colorless juice of the grapes, not their red skins.

✔ **Guardiolo** (gwar-dee-*oh*-lo): Guardiolo Bianco is a dry white made mainly from Malvasia Bianca di Candia and Falanghina; a Rosso and Rosato are mainly Sangiovese. Guardiolo Aglianico is a dry red with at least 90 percent of that variety, and Guardiolo Falanghina is a dry white 90 percent varietal, with Malvasia Bianca and/or other white grapes. A *spumante* is a dry sparkling wine made from the same varieties as the Falanghina.

✔ **Sannio** (*sahn*-nee-oh): This is a new, general wine zone covering the entire Benevento province, as a catch-all designation for wines outside the province's other DOC zones.

Apulia: Italy's wine barrel

Apulia, or Puglia (*poo*-l'yah), as the Italians call it, is truly Italy's wine lake, producing between 100 and 130 million cases of wine annually. About 80 percent of Puglia's wine is red, but less than 4 percent of it is DOC. Most of it is unremarkable wine made by large-volume cooperatives that's shipped north in bulk to improve the less robust red wines of cooler climes.

Puglia boasts three major grape varieties (Negroamaro, Primitivo, and Malvasia Nera) and three notable DOC wines from the following regions:

✔ The Salento Peninsula, the most important area for quality

✔ The "Trulli" district, north of the Salento Peninsula

✔ Central Apulia, including Castel del Monte, a quality zone

The Salento Peninsula

The Salento Peninsula is Puglia's major wine district, and its 11 DOC wines include the renowned Salice Salentino and Primitivo di Manduria. Most of its wines are dark and robust, with ripe flavors and rather high alcohol content. They're made mainly from Negroamaro and/or Primitivo, with Malvasia Nera the third most important grape. (But Aglianico, Campania's noble red grape — and in our opinion the best red variety in Southern Italy — is an emerging presence in the peninsula, either for varietal or, more commonly, blended red wines.)

Here are a couple Salento Peninsula DOC wines of note:

- **Salice Salentino** (*sah*-lee-chae-sah-len-*tee*-no) is Puglia's wine ambassador: It's the one Apulian wine that many winedrinkers abroad have tasted, or at least heard of. It's a dark, robust wine of the South, with all the warm, ripe, even slightly baked, flavors of sun-drenched grapes. It's made mainly from Negroamaro, with up to 20 percent Malvasia Nera. The late Cosimo Taurino, whose wines have had great success on the U.S. market (and whose son, Francesco, continues his work), favored a lusty style for this wine.

- **Primitivo di Manduria** (pre-meh-*tee*-vo-dee-mahn-*doo*-ree-ah) is both the name of a DOC wine and the name of a grape. Of the various types of Primitivo grapes, this is the one thought to be genetically the same as Zinfandel. Primitivo di Manduria wine always comes 100 percent from that grape. It's rich, ripe, and explosively fruity; its minimum alcohol content is 14 percent but usually higher. Although it can age for a few years, it's best young. The Perucci brothers — who make wine under the Pervini (an acronym for "Perucci Vini"), Felline, and Sinfarosa brands—are greatly responsible for the improvement of wines in this DOC zone.

The "Trulli" district

The Trulli district, south of the city of Bari, is an area of valleys and gorges carved by the Itria River. Puglia's most renowned white wine, **Locorotondo** (lo-co-ro-*tohn*-doh), comes from here. It's a dry white made mainly from Verdeca with 35 to 50 percent Bianco di Alessano, and Fiano and/or Bombino Bianco and/or Malvasia Toscana optional. A *spumante* style also exists.

Martina Franca (or **Martina**) is the other white DOC wine of the Trulli district. It's very similar to Locorotondo, with exactly the same grape varieties. Martina Franca, the community at the center of this wine zone, is a dramatic, *trulli* hill town, five miles south of Locorotondo.

Castel del Monte

Castel del Monte is the most important DOC wine in the Bari province of Central Puglia. Castel del Monte's best producer is Rivera, a longstanding leader here, whose Rosso Riserva "Il Falcone" is internationally renowned.

Castel del Monte can be a blended Rosso, Rosato or Bianco wine or one of seven varietal wines. The Rosso is a dry red mainly from Uva di Troia and/or Aglianico and/or Montepulciano, with up to 35 percent other red varieties. The dry Rosato derives from Bombino Nera and/or Aglianico and/or Uva di Troia, and up to 35 percent other red varieties. The Bianco is a dry white mainly from Pampanuto (an indigenous variety) and/or Chardonnay and/or Bombino Bianco, with up to 35 percent other white varieties.

Recommended Puglia producers

Almost all of Puglia's best wines are red, and a large majority of them come from the Salento Peninsula and are based on Negroamaro, Puglia's leading variety — except when they're Primitivo wines. Following are our recommended wine producers in Puglia, listed alphabetically:

- Botromagno
- Candido
- Cantina del Locorotondo
- D'Alfonso del Sordo
- Felline
- Lomazzi & Sarli
- Nugnes
- Masseria Pepe
- Rivera
- Sinfarosa
- Cosimo Taurino
- Agricole Vallone
- Valle dell'Asso
- Conti Zecca

Chapter 5

Pairing Wine with Food

. . . .

In This Chapter
▶ Predictable reactions between wines and foods
▶ Guiding principles and combos for matchmakers

. . . .

*W*ine is meant to go with food. And good food is meant to go with wine. Sounds easy, yet there are thousands of wines in the world, and each one is different. There are also thousands of basic foods in the world, each different — not to mention the infinite combinations of foods in prepared dishes (what we really eat). In reality, food-with-wine is about as simple an issue as boy-meets-girl.

The Dynamics of Food and Wine

Every dish is dynamic — it's made up of several ingredients and flavors that interact to create a (more or less) delicious whole. Every wine is dynamic in exactly the same way. When food and wine combine in your mouth, the dynamics of each change; the result is completely individual to each dish-and-wine combination.

✔ **The food can exaggerate a characteristic of the wine.** For example, if you eat walnuts (which are tannic) with a tannic red wine, such as a Bordeaux, the wine tastes so dry and astringent that most people would consider it undrinkable.

- ✔ **The food can diminish a characteristic of the wine.** Protein diminishes the impression of tannin, for example, and an overly tannic red wine — unpleasant on its own — could be delightful with rare steak or roast beef.

- ✔ **The flavor intensity of the food can obliterate the wine's flavor or vice versa.** If you've ever drunk a big, rich red wine with a delicate filet of sole, you've had this experience firsthand.

- ✔ **The wine can contribute new flavors to the dish.** For example, a red Zinfandel that's gushing with berry fruit can bring its berry flavors to the dish, as if another ingredient had been added.

- ✔ **The combination of wine and food can create an unwelcome third-party flavor that wasn't in either the wine or the food originally.** For instance, we get a metallic flavor when we eat plain white-meat turkey with red Bordeaux.

- ✔ **The food and wine can interact perfectly, creating a sensational taste experience that's greater than the food or the wine alone.** This scenario is what we hope will happen every time we eat and drink, but it's as rare as a show-stopping dish.

What happens between food and wine isn't haphazard. Certain elements of food react in predictable ways with certain elements of wine, giving you a fighting chance at making successful matches. The next sections outline some ways that food and wine interact, based on the components of the wine.

Each wine and each dish has more than one component, and the simple relationships we describe can be complicated by other elements in the wine or the food. Whether a wine is considered tannic, sweet, acidic, or high in alcohol depends on its dominant component.

Tannic wines

Tannic wines include most wines based on the Cabernet Sauvignon grape (including red Bordeaux), Barolo and Barbaresco, and any wine — white or red — that has become tannic from aging in new oak barrels. These wines can

- ✔ Diminish the perception of sweetness in a food

- ✔ Taste softer and less tannic when served with protein-rich, fatty foods, such as steak or cheese

- ✔ Taste less bitter when paired with salty foods

- ✔ Taste astringent, or mouth-drying, when drunk with spicy-hot foods

Sweet wines

Some wines that often have some sweetness include most inexpensive California white wines, White Zinfandel, and many Rieslings (unless they're labeled *dry* or *trocken*). Sweet wines also include dessert wines such as Port, sweetened Sherries, and late-harvest wines. These wines can

- ✔ Taste less sweet, but fruitier, when matched with salty foods

- ✔ Make salty foods more appealing

- ✔ Go well with sweet foods

Acidic wines

Acidic wines include most Italian white wines; Sancerre, Pouilly-Fumé, and Chablis; traditionally made red wines from Rioja; most dry Rieslings; and wines based on Sauvignon Blanc that are fully dry. These wines can

✔ Taste less acidic when served with salty foods or slightly sweet foods

✔ Make foods taste a bit saltier

✔ Counterbalance oily or fatty heaviness in food

High-alcohol wines

High-alcohol wines include many California wines, both white and red; Barolo and Barbaresco; fortified wines such as Port and Sherry; and most wines produced from grapes grown in warm climates. These wines can

✔ Overwhelm lightly flavored or delicate dishes

✔ Go well with slightly sweet foods

Birds of a Feather, or Opposites Attract?

Two principles can help in matching wine with food: the complementary principle and the contrast principle. The complementary principle involves choosing a wine that's similar in some way to the dish you plan to serve; the contrast principle involves combining foods with wines that are dissimilar to them in some way.

The characteristics of a wine that can either resemble or contrast with the characteristics of a dish are

✔ **The wine's flavors:** Earthy, herbal, fruity, vegetal

✔ **The intensity of flavor in the wine:** Weak flavor intensity, moderately flavorful, or very flavorful

✔ **The wine's texture:** Crisp and firm, or soft and supple

✔ **The weight of the wine:** Light-bodied, medium-bodied, or full-bodied

You probably use the complementary principle often without realizing it: You choose a light-bodied wine to go with a light dish, a medium-bodied wine to go with a fuller dish, and a full-bodied wine to go with a heavy dish. Some other examples of the complementary principle in action are

✔ **Dishes with flavors that resemble those in the wine:** Think about the flavors in a dish the same way you think about the flavors in wine — as families of flavors. For instance, if a dish has mushrooms, it has an earthy flavor. Then consider which wines would offer their own earthy flavor. The earthy flavors of white Burgundy complement risotto with mushrooms, for example.

✔ **Foods with texture that's similar to that of the wine:** A California Chardonnay with a creamy, rich texture could match the rich, soft texture of lobster, for example.

✔ **Foods and wines whose intensity of flavor match:** A very flavorful Asian stir-fry or Tex-Mex dish would be at home with a very flavorful, rather than a subtle, wine.

The contrast principle seeks to find flavors or texture in a wine that aren't in a dish but that would enhance it. A dish of fish or chicken in a rich cream and butter sauce, for example, may be matched with a dry Vouvray, a white wine whose crispness (thanks to its uplifting, high acidity) would counterbalance the heaviness of the dish.

You also apply the contrast principle every time you serve simple food, like unadorned lamb chops or hard cheese and bread, with a gloriously complex aged wine.

 In order to apply either principle, you have to have a good idea of what the food is going to taste like and what various wines taste like. That second part can be a real stumbling block for people who don't devote every ounce of their free energy to learning about wine. The solution is to ask your wine merchant. A retailer may not have the world's greatest knack in wine and food pairings (then again, he or she might), but he should at least know what his wines taste like.

Pairing Wisdom of the Ages

In wine-and-food terms, it pays to know the classic pairings because they're a sure thing. Here are some famous and reliable combinations:

- Oysters and traditional, unoaked Chablis
- Lamb and red Bordeaux
- Walnuts and Stilton cheese with Port
- Salmon with Pinot Noir
- Braised beef with Barolo
- Soup and dry amontillado Sherry
- Grilled chicken with Beaujolais
- Goat cheese with Sancerre or Pouilly-Fumé
- Dark chocolate with California Cabernet Sauvignon

Chapter 6

Ten FAQs about Wine

*I*n our years of teaching about wine and helping customers in wine shops, we've noticed that the same questions about wine pop up again and again. Here are our answers.

What's the Best Wine?

There's no single "best wine" for everyone because taste is personal. If you want to drink a good wine that's right for you, you have to first decide what the characteristics of that wine could be. Then get advice from a knowledgeable retailer.

When Should I Drink This Wine?

The great majority of wines are ready to drink when you buy them. Some of them may improve marginally if you hold them for a year or so, but they won't improve enough for you to notice, unless you're a particularly thoughtful and experienced taster.

Some fine wines are an exception: They *need* to age in order to achieve their potential quality. When stored properly, the best red Bordeaux wines, Barolos, Barbarescos, and Brunello di Montalcinos can age for at least 20 years in good vintages. The best white Burgundies improve with at least 10 years of aging, in good vintage years.

Is Wine Fattening?

A glass of dry wine contains 80 to 85 percent water, 12 to 14 percent ethyl alcohol, and small quantities of tartaric acid and various other components. Wine contains no fat.

A 4-ounce serving of dry white wine has about 104 calories, and 4 ounces of red wine has about 110 calories. Sweeter wines contain about 10 percent more calories depending on how sweet they are; fortified wines also contain additional calories due to higher alcohol.

What Grape Variety Made This Wine?

Most New World wines (from the Americas, Australia, and other continents besides Europe) tell you what grape variety they're made from right on the label — it's often the very name of the wine. Traditional European wines blended from several grape varieties usually don't give you that information a) because the winemakers consider the name of the place more important than the grapes and b) because often the grapes they use are local varieties whose names few people would recognize.

Which Vintage Should I Buy?

Most of the time, for most wines, the vintage to buy is the vintage you *can* buy — the current vintage. For white wines, the current vintage represents grapes that were harvested as recently as nine months ago or as long as three years ago, depending on the type of wine; for red wines, the current vintage is a date one to four years ago.

Are There Any Wines without Sulfites?

Sulfur dioxide exists naturally in wine as a result of fermentation. If you wish to limit your consumption of sulfites, dry red wines should be your first choice, followed by dry white wines. Sweet wines contain the most sulfur dioxide.

What Are Organic Wines?

The following categories apply to both domestic wines and imported wines sold in the United States:

- ✔ *Wine made from organically grown grapes;* these are wines whose grapes come from certified organic vineyards.
- ✔ *Organic wine;* these wines come from organically grown grapes and are also produced organically, that is, without the addition of chemical additives such as sulfur dioxide during winemaking.

What Is a Wine Expert?

A wine expert is someone with a high level of knowledge about wine in general, including grape growing, winemaking, and the various wines of the world. A wine expert also has a high degree of skill in tasting wine.

How Do I Know When to Drink My Stored, Older Wines?

No precise answer to this question exists because all wines age at a different pace. Even two bottles of the same wine that are stored under the same conditions can age differently.

If you have a specific wine in mind, contact the winery. In the case of fine, older vintages, the winemaker and his staff are usually happy to give you their opinion on the best time to drink their wine. If you have several bottles of the same wine, try one from time to time to see how the wine is developing. Your own taste is the best guide.

Do Old Wines Require Special Handling?

Like humans, wine can become somewhat fragile in its later years. For one thing, it doesn't like to travel. If you must move old wine, give it several days' rest before opening the bottle. (Red Burgundies and other Pinot Noirs are especially disturbed by journeys.)

Older wines, with their delicate bouquet and flavors, can easily be overwhelmed by strongly flavored foods. Simple cuts of meat or just hard cheeses and good, crusty bread are usually fine companions for mature wines.

 If you're going to drink an older wine, don't over-chill it, whether it's white or red. Older wines show their best at moderate temperatures. Temperatures below 60°F (15.5°C) inhibit development in the glass.